Commitment and Complexity

Jewish Wisdom in an Age of Upheaval

Selections from the Writings of
Rabbi Yehuda Amital

Commitment and Complexity

Jewish Wisdom in an Age of Upheaval

Selections from the Writings of
Rabbi Yehuda Amital

Selected and edited by Aviad Hacohen

Ktav Publishing House, Inc.
Yeshivat Har Etzion

Kaeren Fish, Translator
Reuven Ziegler, Translation Editor

Library of Congress Cataloging-in-Publication Data

Kol Yehudah. English
  Commitment and complexity : Jewish wisdom in an age of upheaval : selections from
the writings of Rabbi Yehuda Amital / selected and edited by Aviad Hacohen ; translated
by Kaeren Fish.
     p. cm.
  This collection was originally published in Hebrew as a tribute to Rav Amital on the
occasion of his eightieth birthday.
  ISBN 978-1-60280-030-4
  1. 'Amital, Yehudah--Teachings. 2. Judaism. 3. Philosophy, Jewish. 4. Jewish ethics.
Hacohen, Aviad. II. Fish, Kaeren. III. Title.
  BM755.A69K6513 2008
  296.3--dc22
                                2008009255

Distributed by
KTAV Publishing House, Inc.
930 Newark Avenue
Jersey City, NJ 07306
Email: bernie@ktav.com
www.ktav.com
(201) 963-9524
Fax (201) 963-0102

In memory of
Fani and Jeno Deutsch
Ilona and Kalman Fulep

Table of Contents

Preface

The teachings of Rav Yehuda Amital cover vast expanses: Halakha and Aggada, Talmud and Midrash, philosophy and morality, life experience and sensible guidance. Their range and diversity reflect striking originality, courage and breadth of knowledge.

On many occasions, when the situation has called for it, Rav Amital has spoken out, in a voice that is clear, pointed, sometimes scathing. He has always taught that "When a person studies Torah and does not hear a cry for help, something is deficient in his study." He would add, "So long as I feel that I am able to say something that will be to the benefit of Torah, to the benefit of the Jewish People or the Land of Israel, I will not refrain from voicing my views. So long as I believe that I am able to diminish *chillul Hashem* (desecration of God's Name) and to increase the glory of Heaven, to bring individuals closer, to save Jews from bloodshed or to save something of the Land of Israel, I have not refrained from voicing my opinion."

The students of Yeshivat Har Etzion have learned a great many lessons from Rav Amital. Many of his teachings have become cherished cornerstones of our worldview. They reflect complexity rather than superficiality and simplicity. "Halakha has come to be perceived, by the youth, as some-thing autistic, unconnected with reality;" "There are no quick fixes in education;" avoiding desecration of God's Name – from all of these emerges the voice of Rav Amital, a voice that is unique, original, authentic and courageous.

I have sought to pluck a few pearls from this great sea, to reflect something of Rav Amital's multi-faceted teachings. This collection of thoughts, ideas and reflections sheds light on his path and his messages, as conveyed to thousands of students, orally and in writing, over the course of several decades.

What we gain by highlighting thoughts and ideas in this manner is matched by what we lose: statements are removed from the general context in which they were uttered, uprooted from the source of their vitality. Anyone seeking to experience their original flavor is obliged to visit them in the panoramic landscape within which they blossomed. Nevertheless, this collection serves the purpose of illuminating various facets of Rav Amital's teachings, weaving their fine threads into a rich tapestry of wisdom, insight, and knowledge.

Most of the contents of this book appear here in English for the first time. Many thanks to Kaeren Fish for her skillful translation. Some selections are taken from material that has already appeared in English in various books and journals published by Yeshivat Har Etzion, under the general editorship of Rabbi Reuven Ziegler. I thank Mark Ginsberg for collating this material, Rabbi Yoseif Bloch for editing the previously unpublished selections, Debra Berkowitz for proofreading, and Rabbi Ziegler for overseeing the production of this entire volume and reviewing its contents. Yeshivat Har Etzion also conveys its gratitude to Mr. Bernard Scharfstein of Ktav Publishing House for his helpfulness and enthusiasm in bringing this volume to print.

This collection was originally published in Hebrew as a tribute to Rav Amital on the occasion of his eightieth birthday. We, his students, wish him continued health and productivity:

> *A righteous man shall flourish like a palm tree;*
> *He grows like a cedar in Lebanon.*
> *Those who are planted in the House of God*
> *Shall flourish in the courts of our God.*
> *They continue to bring forth fruit in old age,*
> *Still ripe and youthful.*
>
> (*Tehillim* 92:13-15)

Aviad Hacohen
Jerusalem, 5768

Am Yisrael

Some people think that the Torah takes precedence over *Am Yisrael*, the Jewish People. This is a mistake. The Torah is not meant to be just "for its own sake," but for the sake of creating a nation with a moral, spiritual character. [*"Am Yisrael* Before *Eretz Yisrael," Sevivot* 22 (5749)]

❧

The "chosen nation" (cf. *Tehillim* 33:12) is a nation which has been entrusted by the Holy One, Blessed be He, with a historical mission, the fulfillment of which will take three or four thousand years. *Am Yisrael* is destined to be "kingdom of priests and a holy nation" (*Shemot* 19:6). Like the mission of the priest vis-à-vis his congregation, so is the mission of *Am Yisrael* vis-à-vis the family of nations. [*"Am Yisrael* before *Eretz Yisrael," Sevivot* 22 (5749)]

❧

Among fairly broad circles, interest in the Jews of the Diaspora is limited to their potential for *aliya*. The fact that what goes on in the State of Israel has an effect on manifestations of antisemitism around the world is ignored. Indeed, antisemitism exists everywhere, but there is a great difference between hatred of Jews that lies beneath the surface and hatred that lifts its head. Clearly, the problem of antisemitism cannot be Israel's sole consideration, but there is no doubt that in its actions, the State must be guided by the effects of antisemitism in the world. Ignoring responsibility for *Am Yisrael* in the Diaspora is unacceptable and dangerous. ["A Political Message or an Educational Message," *Alon Shevut* 100 (5743), 40]

∽o∾

We must remember that there are hundreds of thousands of Jews in the world who have lost any connection with Judaism or the synagogue. Their entire Jewish connection is expressed in their identification with the State of Israel. For them, the question of drawing them close to the State or distancing them from it is a question of life or death, from a Jewish perspective. These Jews are greatly influenced by public opinion in the media, despite the clear knowledge that it is guided by antisemitic tendencies. Therefore, belittling world public opinion is unacceptable and irresponsible, and that's without even mentioning the political influence of world public opinion. ["A Political Message or an Educational Message," *Alon Shevut* 100 (5743), 40]

∽o∾

There is a hierarchy of values in Judaism, and anyone who fails to differentiate *"bein kodesh le-kodesh"* (between one level of holiness and another) will end up unable to differentiate *"bein kodesh le-chol"* (between the holy and the profane), as we say in the *Havdala* prayer. The proper order is: the nation, the Torah, the land. Chazal address the importance of this hierarchy in *Tana De-vei Eliyahu Rabba*, Chapter 14: "He said to me, 'My master, there are two things in my heart which I love greatly – Torah, and [the nation of] Israel, but I do not know which of them takes precedence.' I said to him: 'People usually say that Torah takes precedence over everything else, as it is written: "God acquired me at the beginning of His way" (*Mishlei* 8:22), but I say that the holy [nation of] Israel takes precedence, as it is written, "Israel is holy to God; the first of His produce" (*Yirmiyahu* 2:3).'" The interests of *Am Yisrael* certainly take precedence over the interests of *Eretz Yisrael*. ["A Political Message or an Educational Message," *Alon Shevut* 100 (5743), 42]

Chillul Hashem and *Kiddush Hashem*

The Name of God is desecrated (*chillul Hashem*) when a person who studied Torah fails to relate to other people in a fitting manner. The sanctification of His Name (*kiddush Hashem*) is just the opposite – it takes place when the Name of Heaven becomes beloved through him. The Sages teach us that the Name of Heaven becomes beloved not only when one produces articles, debates, and sermons, but first and foremost, when one serves as a role model of moral and humane behavior, which generates admiration and emulation by others. A special obligation falls upon students of Torah to make the Name of Heaven beloved to other people. [*Jewish Values*, 150]

❧

If it is generally true that a Torah scholar is obligated to cause God's name to become beloved, this applies all the more in a generation in which so many have abandoned the way of Torah and *mitzvot*. This is especially true in Israel, where the tension between the religious and non-religious worlds expresses itself in political contexts as well, and the media often present the negative aspects of the observant community. In our day, the best way to establish lines of communication with the non-religious is through conduct that sanctifies God's name. Debating the issues is usually ineffective; the best way to draw people close to Torah is by way of personal example. [*Jewish Values*, 151]

❧

I believe that we merited a Jewish state only because of God's desire to sanctify His Name in the aftermath of the terrible desecration of His Name during the Holocaust. The establishment of the State and its victories in war against the Arab armies that rose up against it constitute a response of sanctification of God's Name. Precisely for this reason, the obligation to sanctify God's Name has special significance in our time for those of us who live in the State of Israel, the entire establishment of which stemmed from this principle. This is why, on various occasions over the years, I have felt obligated to protest against instances of the desecration of God's Name. This was the only cause for which I felt a need to speak out publicly. [*Jewish Values*, 155]

∽∘∾

The sin committed [in Baruch Goldstein's massacre at the Cave of the Patriarchs] against the sons of Yishmael, the son of Avraham, is only one side of the coin. The other side shows a terrible transgression against God and against the Torah, whose "ways are ways of pleasantness, and all of its paths are peace" (*Mishlei* 3:17). Who dares to garb the Torah and its commandments in such cruelty and ugliness? It has become clear that not only Islam but also the fringe element of Orthodox Jewry is capable of producing terrorists with skullcaps. Not enough has been done, among the students and teachers of Torah, to uproot such false thoughts and ideas. ["Terrorism with a Skullcap," *Ve-eleh Shenot…* (Tel Aviv, 5757), 309]

∽∘∾

Baruch Goldstein besmirched the Jewish nation and the Torah with the disgrace of spilling innocent blood. Beyond the moral and religious baseness of killing innocent people as they knelt in prayer, the terrible murder caused a desecration of God's Name in the eyes of the entire world. Perhaps Goldstein perpetrated this massacre specifically because he viewed it as an act of "wiping out Amalek" (*Devarim* 25:19), out of a sense of dehumanization of every Arab. Our Sages recognized long ago that the entire Torah, when given over into the wrong hands, may become "a potion of death" (*Ta'anit* 7a). But it would have been difficult to imagine that a mass murder could be perpetrated in the name of the Torah, concerning which the Rambam wrote that "the judgments of the Torah do not bring vengeance into the world; rather, they bring compassion and kindness and peace into the world" (*Hilkhot Shabbat* 2:3). ["Terrorism with a Skullcap," *Ve-eleh Shenot...* (Tel Aviv, 5757), 309]

Commitment

Freedom from responsibility is not unique to our society. It exists in other places as well, particularly in Western countries. However, in our compact society, replete as it is with political, religious, ethnic and social tensions, its effect is destructive in the extreme. The placement of liberal individualism as a central pillar of our culture, coupled with the ranking of the rights of the individual at the top of our scale of values, has led to the prevalent sense of freedom from commitment. The very notion of commitment to a cause or an object runs contrary to the concept of freedom. Therefore any commitment – whether to the nation, the state, society, or to one's spouse and family – has no place in an era of freedom of the individual. To my mind, this sense of freedom from commitment constitutes a significant factor in the decrease of motivation in the army. ["The Social Challenges Confronting the State of Israel," *Alei Etzion* 10 (5761), 9-11]

∽○∾

One of the most important challenges today is to educate towards commitment: commitment to the nation, to the family, to society, to the state, and to Judaism's world of values. ["The Social Challenges Confronting the State of Israel," *Alei Etzion* 10 (5761), 12]

Complexity

Simplistic thinking must be avoided. A person must fight against superficiality and understand the complexity of the world; one must know that not everything in the world is black or white – most of it is gray. It is not easy to understand the gray, but the ability to understand human complexity requires that attention be paid to such cases as well. The development of such sensitivity is important not only for understanding other people. It also helps a person acquire a more profound perspective upon reality, historical events, and ideologies, one that goes beyond the formal view, which often leads to a superficial way of looking at things. [*Jewish Values*, 170-171]

∽◦∾

Simplistic thought – seeing issues as black-and-white, and an inability to perceive a whole and complex picture – has become a national epidemic. The media continually broadcast simple and uncomplicated messages. There is no time for involved explanations which require more air-time. The media prefer to emphasize the extremes, the black and white, the unequivocal, almost ruling out anything in-between, anything gray or complex. There are no doubts. The expression "without any doubt" is repeated over and over by those interviewed. A situation has been created whereby simplistic thought has not only gained legitimacy but has become the accepted language even among circles which have pretensions as to the importance of their own opinions. ["The Social Challenges Confronting the State of Israel," *Alei Etzion* 10 (5761), 13]

∽∘∾

Using complex thought, the religious person is able to understand the point of view of the secular person, and vice versa. In such a situation the demands of each side towards the other side decrease. Each side understands that things which are obvious to them are not necessarily obvious to the other; sometimes they are even completely unintelligible. In the absence of such an approach, statements about openness are simply meaningless. The same can be said of the relationship between the political left and right. When one appreciates the complexity of Israel's situation, then one is able to recognize the legitimacy of each political opinion. We have reached a situation where simplistic thought is increasing the polarization of society and leading to an inability to listen to others – to the extent of delegitimization of other opinions. The distance between delegitimization and demonization is not all that great. And we have unfortunately been witness to the dangers of demonization of the other opinion in the tragic assassination of a Prime Minister. ["The Social Challenges Confronting the State of Israel," *Alei Etzion* 10 (5761), 14]

Controversy

It is not enough to distance oneself from a place of strife; one must run away from it. A person cannot maintain himself and stand on the side while controversy rages around him. In my opinion, this is a very important consideration; it is better for a person to suffer substantial loss, rather than remain in a workplace marked by strife. The Gemara in *Chullin* (89a) states: "Rabbi Ila'a said: The world exists only for one who keeps silent (*bolem*) during a quarrel, as it says (*Iyyov* 26:7): 'He hangs the earth on nothing (*beli-ma*).'" The world does not exist by the merit of people of action who disagree and argue about everything, but rather by the merit of those who successfully avoid controversy and strife. It is particularly important to avoid strife that is "for the sake of Heaven," regarding which there are no constraints, because a person thinks that everything is permitted to him, being that he is acting – in his own estimation – for the sake of Heaven. [*Jewish Values*, 211-212]

Da'at Torah

Today it goes almost without saying: even some adherents of religious Zionism, suffering from an inferiority complex, go looking for *da'at Torah*, an authoritative rabbinic imprimatur for every decision. In the sources – the Rambam, the *Shulchan Arukh* or the other halakhic authorities – there is no hint of the idea that in spheres that are not halakhic, it is necessary to consult with a rabbinical authority. ["What is the Biblical Source for the Concept of *Da'at Torah*?", *Alon Shevut Bogrim* 12 (5758), 100]

∾∘∾

Where I was born and lived until the age of eighteen, we never heard of any such concept as *"da'at Torah."* Obviously, when it came to questions of Halakha, people would consult a rabbi. It was not unusual for a rabbi to voice his opinion, quite unequivocally, on moral questions, too. But as to the idea that all communal matters must be decided by a rabbi – there was no such thing. This is a new phenomenon. ["What is the Biblical Source for the Concept of *Da'at Torah*?", *Alon Shevut Bogrim* 12 (5758), 100]

∾∘∾

Let there be no doubt: it is a mitzva to respect Torah scholars. However, I believe that I show no disrespect for [ultra-Orthodox leader] Rav Schach if I do not consult him regarding worldly matters. In our times, people don't consider a Torah scholar to be genuine unless he performs some "wonder" or reveals sparks of "divine inspiration." Some years ago, I expressed an opinion on a certain matter. Immediately I came under attack: "But Rav Zvi Yehuda Kook said otherwise! How can you say something that contradicts his opinion? Is that the way of Torah?" Is Rav Zvi Yehuda the *Urim ve-Tummim*, the oracle worn by the *Kohen Gadol* (High Priest)? Why does he have to be followed on all matters? We have common sense, and we have to follow its dictates. This in no way affects the mitzva to respect Torah scholars – concerning which, unfortunately, people are not always sufficiently careful. ["What is the Biblical Source for the Concept of *Da'at Torah*?", *Alon Shevut Bogrim* 12 (5758), 101]

Derekh Eretz

Yiddish has a unique term, used by speakers of other languages as well, that is very difficult to translate – *"menschlichkeit."* The Hebrew term *derekh eretz* is only roughly equivalent. Paraphrasing the expression in the *Siddur*, "One should always be a man who fears God in private as well as in public" (*"Le-olam yehe adam…"*), Jews in eastern Europe used to say: "One should always be a man (*mensch*)." That is, first one must be a *mensch*; afterwards, one can fear God. The Torah reinforces and deepens the idea of *menschlichkeit*, but this quality is demanded of man even before he acquires Torah. [*Jewish Values*, 131]

∽o∾

One who engages in Torah study is expected to be meticulous not only about explicit *halakhot*, but also about conducting himself in a manner of *derekh eretz* in his relations with other people. The Mishna in *Avot* (3:12) states: "Rabbi Yishmael said: Be submissive to a superior and kindly to the young; and receive all people cheerfully." The Rambam's remarks, in his commentary to the Mishna (ad loc.), are very significant from a human perspective: "It is fitting to receive every person, lowly and grand, free-man and slave, every member of the human race, with joy and happiness." This goes beyond what Shammai says (*Avot* 1:15): "Receive all people with a kindly countenance." This is a unique expression of *derekh eretz* – the duty to receive all people not only with a kindly countenance, but with joy and happiness. According to Rabbi Naftali Zvi Yehuda Berlin (the Netziv), in the introduction to his commentary to the Torah, *Ha'amek Davar*, the virtue of the Patriarchs lay in the way they behaved with *derekh eretz* even towards idolaters: "This was the praise of the Patriarchs, that in addition to being righteous, saintly and lovers of God in the best possible manner, they were also straight and honest; that is, they conducted themselves with the nations of the world, even the ugliest idolaters, with love, and they sought their welfare, that being the fulfillment of the purpose of creation." [*Jewish Values*, 132-133]

∽o∾

The importance attached to *derekh eretz* by our Sages sharply contrasts with the widespread phenomenon in which people are meticulous in observing the minutiae of Halakha and even supererogatory stringencies, but they are careless when it comes to *menschlichkeit*. Moreover, their very insistence on excessive halakhic stringency often leads to violations of the rules of *derekh eretz*. Our rabbis teach us that *derekh eretz* is a value of great weight, one that can override various stringencies. [*Jewish Values*, 133-134]

Diaspora

One of the most important challenges facing Israel in the future will be the question of how to help the Diaspora in its desperate battle for survival. The time has come to change our agenda. Instead of looking for ways in which Israel can benefit from the assistance of the Diaspora, we have to look for ways in which Israel can help Diaspora Jewry. ["The Social Challenges Confronting the State of Israel," *Alei Etzion* 10 (5761), 18]

∽०∾

If we wish to maintain the historical continuity of the Jewish nation, something which I am certain that the vast majority of the nation does indeed want, then we have to emphasize the fact of our Jewishness. The best way of doing this is to express our commitment and responsibility towards the Jewish nation, wherever they may be scattered. Only in this way will we find the gates of our rich Jewish heritage opened before us. ["The Social Challenges Confronting the State of Israel," *Alei Etzion* 10 (5761), 18]

∽०∾

The Land of Israel belongs to all Jews in the world. If it is decreed, God forbid, that we are to suffer in *Eretz Yisrael* because of our sins, then we suffer not only because of the sins of those who live here, but because of the sins of all Jews, wherever they may be. The State of Israel has a responsibility towards Jews wherever they are – whether they are Shabbat-observant or whether they desecrate Shabbat; whether they are considering *aliya* or whether they have no such intention. To the extent that the State of Israel seeks to remain true to its destiny, it is obligated constantly to transmit educational messages to the Jewish world about faith, Torah, and morality. That is our destiny; that is our task. ["A Political Message or an Educational Message," *Alon Shevut* 100 (5743), 43]

∾◦∾

We often speak about the danger facing *Eretz Yisrael ha-shelema* (the complete Land of Israel), but we hear almost nobody expressing concern as to the danger facing "*Am Yisrael ha-shalem*" (the complete Jewish People). A land that is destroyed may be rebuilt in the future. But a nation that is destroyed – with thousands of its members disappearing from Judaism every year, embodying the verse (*Mishlei* 2:19), "All who go there will not return" – is there any hope of bringing them back? ["A Political Message or an Educational Message," *Alon Shevut* 100 (5743), 50]

Divine Providence

A Jew who believes that events touching on the life of *Am Yisrael* are guided by Divine Providence, will naturally inquire as to their meaning and significance. The Torah and the prophets command us unceasingly to pay attention. It is also a natural intellectual inquiry for one based in faith. If events pass one by without one attempting to penetrate the depth of their true meaning, the Sages consider such a person dead. "A wicked person is considered dead even during his lifetime, since he sees the sun rise but does not recite the blessing 'Who creates the lights;' he sees it setting, but does not recite the blessing 'Who brings evenings'" (*Midrash Tanchuma, Ve-Zot ha-Berakha* 12). Clearly, we do not have the tools to know the secrets of God and to know the considerations, motives and intentions of Divine Providence, "for My thoughts are not your thoughts" (*Yeshayahu* 55:8). However, this does not exempt us from our obligation to observe and to delve. It is Torah, and we must study it (cf. *Berakhot* 62a). ["The Significance of the Yom Kippur War," *Ha-Ma'alot mi-Ma'amakim,* 11]

Eastern Philosophy

Over the last generation, various doctrines originating in the Far East have penetrated the Western world. Modern Western man lives his life in great tension. Under the influence of Eastern teachings, many have begun to advocate a life of tranquility and meditation. Some have seen in this the ideal of human redemption – the ability to reach internal tranquility. I harbor fundamental reservations regarding such approaches. There are certainly people who at times live their lives in excessive tension; they need help to reduce their tension levels. But turning tranquility into a way of life is misguided on several counts. First of all, such an approach is liable to hinder a person who strives for advancement and development in his life. There is a certain contradiction between aspiring for tranquility and positive ambition, the force that drives one to advance and develop himself. Second, directing one's life towards internal tranquility involves egotism, for this is often accompanied by disregard for the problems and needs of society. I especially dissociate myself from such an approach when it comes to the worship of God. [*Jewish Values*, 107]

Education

Regarding Torah study, it is stated: "With my whole heart I have sought You; let me not wander from Your commandments" (*Tehillim* 119:10). The personal element is important even in Torah study; one can express the "understanding of his heart" even when one reaches a halakhic conclusion identical to that of others. Torah study is indeed based upon logic and reasoning, but nonetheless, it is not the same as mathematics, for example, where there can be only one possible conclusion. Rather, the Torah allows for different possible ways of understanding it. [*Jewish Values*, 67]

∽∘∾

Every educational institution, by its very nature, has a built-in problem: the student knows who is teaching him, and the teacher knows whom he is teaching. This situation – direct education, of which both sides are fully conscious – frequently generates resistance on the part of the student against accepting the teacher's world outlook and moral admonitions. This situation is liable to hurt the teacher as well: knowing that he is serving as a role model, he may conduct himself in an unnatural manner. The greatest educational impact is achieved when the teacher is unaware that he is teaching and the student is unaware that he is learning. This is the meaning of "the Name of Heaven shall become beloved through you" (*Yoma* 86a) – a person through his ordinary conduct should bring about a sanctification of God's Name, without even being aware that he is influencing others through his behavior. [*Jewish Values*, 150-151]

Enthusiasm

There are people whose hearts are filled with enthusiasm, encompassed by the raging flames and wild storms of powerful emotions. They give expression to their feelings in the way they live. On the other hand, there are people whose hearts are filled with fire and storms, but they are able to store and contain it within their souls. Outwardly they are quiet, but their hearts are turbulent. "How beautiful are your footsteps (*fe'amayikh*) in shoes" (*Shir Ha-shirim* 7:2) – the word "*fe'amayikh*" is related to the idea of "*pe'imot lev*" – heartbeats, indicating inner enthusiasm. "How beautiful" they are when they are "in shoes" – i.e., when they act within a rhythm, order, precision and discipline. Concerning the idiom, "A coin for a word, two for silence" (*Megilla* 18a), the Rebbe of Ruzhin taught that the word which one feels obligated to say is worth only one coin if is verbalized, but if held in one's heart, in silence, its value doubles. ["In Memory of David Mallick," *Le-David Ha-Alon Ha-Shevi'i* (5745), 81]

Eretz Yisrael

Often I have appeared odd in the eyes of my peers. I have spoken about concerns for the long term. In a generation of "now-ism," it is difficult to speak of the long term. "I have not hidden my face from shame and spitting" (*Yeshayahu* 50:6); nevertheless, "The Lord God helps me, therefore I have not been confounded; therefore I set my face like flint and I know that I shall not be humiliated" (*ibid.* 50:7). The greatest hurt was when people suggested that I am deficient in my love of *Eretz Yisrael*, God forbid. I was connected to *Eretz Yisrael* long before I knew the famous teaching of the Ramban (regarding the mitzva to settle the Land of Israel; Commentary to *Bamidbar* 33:53). When we were liberated from a Nazi labor camp, there was a group of about twenty of us Jews there. We had no newspapers, no radio; we didn't know what was happening in the world. But I said, "I'm going to *Eretz Yisrael*." They said to me, "Are you crazy? You don't know what's going on there!" But I answered, "I'm going." For me, *Eretz Yisrael* is not only a spiritual matter, not just a matter of sanctity. I feel it is my homeland in the simplest sense, and I'm not ashamed of it. ["Hearing the Baby's Cry," *Alon Shevut Bogrim* 1 (5754), 83]

৵৹৵

When my family and I commemorate the day upon which I came to Israel, I combine thanksgiving for being saved from the Nazis with thanksgiving for my *aliya* (immigration to Israel). Indeed, in my mind, the two are intrinsically connected. I did not see myself as gaining total salvation when I had escaped from the Nazis; I only came to view my salvation as complete when I arrived in Israel. I remember that when I took leave of my father – he was forced to remain in the ghetto, while I had received a deportation order to a labor camp – both he and I had absolutely no doubt that we would never meet again in this world. At that time, my father said to me, "I hope that you will get to *Eretz Yisrael*." This was the supreme expression of hope for salvation. [*A World Built*, 133]

∞∞

I could not allow myself to give expression to the feeling that I had no hope of ever seeing my parents alive again. Yet, I did not want to give my parents any hint that such thoughts resided within me. I took leave of my parents with a heavy heart and went to the labor camp. All that I took with me was a small *Tanakh* (Bible), Mishna, and a booklet written by Rabbi Kook. I admit to you today, that during those days I was very pessimistic. Many doubts gnawed at my heart. I only hoped I could die in *Eretz Yisrael*, even if I did not live there. [*A World Built*, 133-134]

∞∞

The importance of *Eretz Yisrael* is not dependent on any outline of its borders, but rather in its being a platform for sovereignty, for kingship, for a State; a platform for the realization of the personality of the individual and of the collective. Our people's destiny is to be "a light to the nations" (*Yeshayahu* 49:6), not as singular individuals, but as a "singular nation" (*Devarim* 7:6). Beyond the day-to-day social, economic and military problems, we must be an ethical example, a moral example. *Eretz Yisrael* is meant to be the land of an exemplary Jewish society. [*"Am Yisrael* before *Eretz Yisrael," Sevivot* 22 (5749)]

∽o∽

My association with *Eretz Yisrael* is one that was ingrained in me from early childhood. My family had been in the process of moving before the war came upon us. Even during my earliest years, *Eretz Yisrael* and the hope of the Messianic redemption were a very tangible and real part of my life.

Let me try to relate one of the most memorable occasions of my childhood. I must have been only four or five, but I still remember everything with total clarity. We were in *cheder* (grade school) and playing in the yard. Suddenly, I saw a great ball of fire come out of the sky – I guess I must have been gifted with an active imagination. I told my friends what I had seen, and we decided that this was a sign that the *Mashiach* (Messiah) was coming! The whole *cheder* became very excited. What do children do when they expect the *Mashiach*? We all ran together to the water tap in the yard and washed our hands in order to purify ourselves for the arrival of the *Mashiach*! I can still remember the rush and the crowd at the water tap. There was an old, gnarled tree in the yard and we began to dance around it and sing. [*A World Built*, 135-136]

∽o∽

My beard has still not turned white with age, and yet during the course of my life I have seen, as our Sages have said, "a world built, destroyed and rebuilt" (*Midrash Lekach Tov, Bereshit* 6:9). I have seen Jews being led to Auschwitz; I have seen Jews dance at the establishment of the State of Israel; I have seen the great victories of the Six-Day War; I have traveled with soldiers to the Suez Canal. I have lived through an epoch, in the shortest span of time. It is hard to believe that in such a short lifetime one could witness so many changes.

Today, the State of Israel stands at the focal point of world history. It is clear that we are living in a period of great change and, as such, it demands of us great deeds. It necessitates sacrifice; it hungers for creativity; it requires accomplishment; it compels us to take action.

From day to day, from year to year, changes take place. To live in such a period, to really and truly live it; to see and understand the dynamics and intensity of Jewish history as it unfolds before us; to gaze upon the great events – upon each one, in and of itself, and upon all of them combined – while we maintain the correct perspective, knowing that it is just a part of the whole; to sense the process of redemption as it unfolds before our very eyes; to know our responsibility in this world, at this time and in this place; to perceive what it is that God demands of us, here and now – all this creates a grave responsibility which one can neither escape nor ignore.

I am the man, poor in worthy deeds, who has seen communities in desolation, and who has merited to behold a land rebuilt: sorrow and sighing, while I was upon a strange and foreign land; gladness and joy, when I came up to Jerusalem. "I will declare Your Name to my brethren; in the midst of a congregation, I will praise You" (*Tehillim* 22:23).

This is God's promise: "For a small moment I have forsaken you, but with great mercies I will gather you" (*Yeshayahu* 54:7). One thing remains clear: "Upon Mount Zion, there will be a remnant" (*Ovadya* 1:17). [*A World Built*, 139-140]

∽᳇᳆∾

In the realm of ethics and values, the crux of the argument concerns the question of whether, in the composite of *Am Yisrael*, Torah, and *Eretz Yisrael*, no one value has more weight than another, or whether we must have a hierarchy of values in which *Am Yisrael* rates highest. The very principle of a hierarchy of holy values, with one higher than the next, is a fundamental one in Torah and in Halakha, as set forth at the beginning of Tractate *Kelim* (1:6-9). The need to arrange a hierarchy of values arises from the fact that in reality, it is not always possible to fully realize all three values. Sometimes the implementation of one value conflicts with another. To those who claim that "*Eretz Yisrael* is in danger," we counter that "*Am Yisrael* is in danger," and that the value of *Am Yisrael* takes precedence over the value of *Eretz Yisrael*. ["Challenges of a New Reality," *Alon Shevut Bogrim* 1 (5754), 73]

∽᳇᳆∾

With the undermining of the dominant extremist view, there are already signs pointing to the end of religious Zionism. We hear talk about the failure of Zionism, and on the nationalist radio station Arutz Sheva, there are already those who speak of the end of Zionism altogether. It is but a short jump from here to a hermetic isolation of the *Dati-*

Leumi community and its psychological distancing from the secular public, claiming that "the argument is not over *Eretz Yisrael*, but rather between Judaism and Hellenism," and asserting that "support for the [Oslo] Accords springs from a life without values." Meanwhile, the public as a whole is in a state of spiritual perplexity. Perplexity is not a vacuum, and it is likely to lead to a wave of youth heading in every possible direction: to Benei Berak, and – in a very different way – to Dizengoff and the beach, and even to New York. ["Challenges of a New Reality," *Alon Shevut Bogrim* 1 (5754), 74]

～०～

It is astounding how the vision of redemption espoused by Rabbi Avraham Yitzchak Kook, *zt"l*, the crux of which was the spiritual revival of *Am Yisrael* in its return to the land, has become limited, in recent years – among those who regard themselves as his students and disciples – to the commandment of settling the land exclusively. Everyone should take a look at his masterwork *Orot* and note how much space is taken up by the subject of *Eretz Yisrael* (not to speak of the specific issue of the boundaries of the land), as opposed to the subject of "the spiritual reawakening of *Am Yisrael*." Interestingly, the nation's moral and spiritual deterioration since the Six-Day War has created no crisis for those who lived in a messianic euphoria; only the possibility of a territorial withdrawal creates such perplexity and crisis. This is a truly puzzling phenomenon. ["Challenges of a New Reality," *Alon Shevut Bogrim* 1 (5754), 74]

～०～

One cannot simply dismiss any opinion that is different and anyone who does not think like everyone else. I, for example, am considered a great heretic because I do not believe that it is forbidden to relinquish so much as a centimeter of *Eretz Yisrael* even when human life is at stake. All of the religious Zionist rabbis today subscribe to this prohibition, while I think differently. I am considered an even greater heretic because, in my view, it is worth relinquishing parts of *Eretz Yisrael* in order to rid ourselves of the yoke of two million Arabs who will join the other million Arabs [who are Israeli citizens], while the number of Jews in the country stands at a mere four-and-a-half million. I do not try to influence anyone. I do not attempt to sell my wares – neither within the yeshiva nor anywhere else. But one has to know that there are people who think differently; one can't just dismiss everything. ["The Significance of the Teachings of Rav Kook for Our Generation," *Alon Shevut Bogrim* 8 (5756), 138]

A war over *Eretz Yisrael* is a war over Jerusalem. ["The Significance of the Yom Kippur War," *Ha-Ma'alot mi-Ma'amakim*, 19]

The Holy One, Blessed be He, chose *Eretz Yisrael* as the territory in which the nation chosen for a mission would realize its essence. In it, the Jewish nation must establish "a kingdom of priests" (*Shemot* 19:6) – not a kingdom like that of the monks in Tibet, but rather a kingdom of priests that assumes responsibility towards the international community. This is the fundamental connection between the land and the nat on. [*"Am Yisrael* before *Eretz Yisrael," Sevivot* 22 (5749)]

∽○∾

Three central values shape my world-view: *Am Yisrael*, Torah and Judaism, and *Eretz Yisrael*. Presenting the settlement of *Eretz Yisrael* as a supreme value is, to my mind, a grave mistake that does not express the spirit of the Torah. We must ensure a durable peace and obtain guarantees for the security of the State of Israel. We must protect the areas of settlement in Yehuda and Shomron (the West Bank), but at the same time we have to ensure the Jewish character of the State of Israel. We face a difficult demographic problem, and we must draw a distinction between different types of settlements. We have no interest in areas that are densely populated by Arabs. We must repeat to ourselves, reiterating and emphasizing, that peace is an important value – one of the fundamental values of Judaism. ["Towards Peace," *Davar*, 11.9.1988]

∽○∾

The connection between the nation of Israel and its land was created differently from that of any other nation. In the natural course of events, the connection between a nation and its land is created after people have lived in a certain area for a long time, have fought for it, have lived through shared experiences and troubles. For us, everything is different. Our connection to our land was created before the first Jew had set foot on it! "And God said to Avram, 'Go out from your country, from your birthplace, from your

father's house, to the land I shall show you'" (*Bereshit* 12:1).
It was then that the connection was formed. This was a
unique event; it has no parallel in history. ["This is the Day
that God Has Made; We Shall Be Happy and Rejoice in It,"
Alon Shevut Bogrim 3 (5754), 93]

∽◦∽

The hawkish, militant line that has become the dominant
line within certain circles of religious Judaism is not only
opposed to the way of Torah, the spirit of Judaism and the
way of religious Jewry since the renewal of the Jewish community in *Eretz Yisrael*, but also causes great damage to the
strengthening of the "*Eretz Yisrael* consciousness" amongst
the nation. Ultimately, this line weakens the willingness of
the nation to fight when put to the test. ["A Political
Message or an Educational Message," *Alon Shevut* 100
(5743), 49]

∽◦∽

The whole view that maintains that all problems, concerns
or suspicions are nullified, or at least dwarfed, where the
wholeness of *Eretz Yisrael* is concerned, is unacceptable to
us. When this view is expressed as a religious, halakhic
approach, we regard this not merely as a distortion, but
also – for our many sins – as a desecration of God's Name.
["The Nation Grows Mighty While Its Discourse Grows
Weak," *Ammudim* 563 (5753), 205]

Eulogy

Our hearts are torn in eight places [referring to Yeshivat Har Etzion's eight fallen students in the Yom Kippur War], tears that cannot be repaired. Our cry, bursting out from the walls of our hearts, is as silent as the cry of every stone of the walls of our *beit midrash*. Where is the lamenter who can express our mourning? Who can count our tears? Who can measure our pain? "Their heart cried out to God: O wall of the daughter of Zion, let your tears run down like a river, day and night; give yourself no rest, let the apple of your eye not let up" (*Eikha* 2:18). ["On the Death of a Son," *Alon Shevut* 17 (5734), 11]

∽o∾

My teachers and rabbis!

I do not mean by this to address the group that has gathered here, at the cemetery – may you all live long lives. I address myself to our friends who are buried here, to them and to their friends, in their hundreds and thousands, buried here and in cemeteries elsewhere, for eternal rest. To them I call out: My teachers and rabbis! Obviously, I mean this in the sense of which Rabbi Chanina spoke (*Ta'anit* 7a): "I have learned much from my teachers; and from my friends – even more than from my teachers; and from my students – the most." I am talking about the sense that everyone can identify with: the parents, the brothers and sisters, the family members, friends. When the seal is broken, the true character of these sons and friends is revealed to us, and their entire personality is exposed before us, in full and in all its glory. The "eight princes" (*Mikha* 5:4) – and, like them, the other students of the yeshiva who have fallen in Israel's wars and in other attacks – they live on in me. The Holy One, Blessed be He, Who knows our thoughts, Who examines hearts and reveals the innermost hidden things – He knows and is witness to what extent those fragments of memory have seeped and been internalized into my personality and my consciousness. For thirty years I have tried to pass them onward; in things that I have written, in things that I have said; in sermons, in classes. And it all lives on as though it was said just yesterday. Therefore, they themselves are my teachers and rabbis. And my soul is bound up with their soul. [Eulogy Delivered on the Day Following Yom Kippur 5764, at the Military Cemetery]

∽ͻo∾

Each one of the fallen princes had a special melody of his own. And it continues to play inside of me, inside my heart, inside your hearts, among all those who knew and know and remember them. Do not belittle that! It is no consolation, but it is something. I lived through the Holocaust, in which millions of Jews lost their lives. Some of them were lost, and the book of their remembrances was lost along with them. We remained but a few, but our book of remembrances is with us, living and life-giving. And we carry it with us, every day, every hour. Every time we open this "book of remembrance," the images and personalities of those "princes of men" come back to us, and give life – to us and to them. "Place me as a seal upon your heart" (*Shir ha-Shirim* 8:6) – the seal is removed, the book is opened, and the pain sears. But the memory of pain has the ability to mold our personality, to enrich us, to nourish us – every day, at any time, at any hour. Perhaps we can give a new meaning to the well-used expression, "*Yehi zikhram barukh*, May their memory be blessed." Their memory lives among us, truly blessed, and it gives us life, and the strength to continue. [Eulogy Delivered on the Day Following Yom Kippur 5764, at the Military Cemetery]

Faith

Sometimes a person is privileged in that when he observes events through lenses of faith, the fog is dispersed and things become clear, and he arrives at a sense of inner certainty – a certainty that may not always be scientifically proven, but whose power is in no way thereby diminished. This is the power of faith – the portion of the servants of God, believers who are the descendants of believers. ["On the Significance of the Yom Kippur War," *Ha-Ma'alot mi-Ma'amakim*, 11]

Family

One of the most important values in Judaism is family, especially in contemporary society which is marked by great alienation and distance between one person and the next. One of the most difficult problems of our times is when people prioritize their career over their family, a phenomenon which unfortunately leads to the break-up of families and other serious difficulties. The value of family cannot be expressed solely through the connection that is felt in the heart; it requires that people devote time to their families, to their spouses and children, at all ages. A person must share his experiences with the other members of his family, experiences which cause him satisfaction as well as his problems – at every age, in accordance with the particular person's understanding – so that his work hours will not be construed as time in which he is totally cut off from his family. [*Jewish Values*, 212-213]

∽∘∾

A person should not develop his career at the expense of his family. A person's family must be of primary importance, and his craft – his profession – must be secondary. This is especially important in our time, when a person's economic and social advancement is dependent in great part on the amount of time that he invests in his work. A clear contradiction often develops between a person's opportunity to advance in his workplace and his ability to invest the appropriate amount of time in his family. This is why it is important to internalize the importance of family. It should be emphasized that the value of family does not mean only giving to one's family, for a person also receives from his family. A person who has a warm and supportive family fares better in the face of all kinds of problems. [*Jewish Values*, 214-215]

Fear of God

Observant Jews generally define themselves as God-fearing people. We therefore tend to identify any religious sentiment with the fear of God. "Religiosity" and "the fear of God" are indeed related, but the two concepts are not identical. There is no clearer expression of "religiosity" than the observance of *mitzvot*: a person who takes a *lulav* on Sukkot fulfills a religious obligation. But he does not fulfill thereby the mitzva of fearing God. [*Jewish Values*, 1]

∽◦∾

The fear of God is characterized by two elements. First, the fear of God requires spiritual effort accompanied by a profound and continuous process. Second, the fear of God requires wisdom and study. The fear of God is the cornerstone of our lives, without which nothing else is truly real. We must, therefore, internalize the idea that when we talk about the fear of God, we are not dealing with something that is easily attained through the observance of *mitzvot* alone. The fear of God is a high level of perfection that can be acquired only through a great investment of intellectual and emotional energy. [*Jewish Values*, 1-3]

Framework and Content

"If the Court and all of Israel see it, and the witnesses were questioned, but they did not manage to declare *'Mekuddash!'* until it was dark, it is a leap-month" (Mishna *Rosh ha-Shana* 3:1). Even if the Court and all of the people witness the sliver of the new moon, and it seems to everyone that the situation is quite clear and that the previous month has already ended, Halakha teaches us that the legal framework and technicalities are binding. If the Court did not manage to declare the new month *"mekuddash"* – sanctified – before nightfall, only the next day will be the start of the new month. There are two dangers that lurk with regard to relation between content and framework. On one hand, among shallow people with a superficial approach, there is the danger of complete adherence to the framework, with forgetfulness of and disdain for the substance. On the other hand, for the idealists who delve deeply and seek out substance, there is the danger of scorning the framework. Our Sages describe the failure of Nadav and Avihu, who were close to God ("I shall be sanctified among those close to Me," *Vayikra* 10:3); they God's friends, as it were. They entered the Tabernacle without the proper attire, without washing their hands and feet (*Midrash Tanchuma, Parashat Acharei Mot* 7). In their great enthusiasm, they scorned the framework, the technicalities. Indeed, a tunic is nothing but an external garment; washing hands and feet is no more than a formal requirement. The important thing is purity of heart, a person's intentions, one's burning desire to stand and minister before God. But our Sages teach us that content that is devoid of any framework is a "foreign fire before God" (*Bamidbar* 3:4). ["'On Aharon's Heart' – In Memory of Aharaleh Friedman, *z"l*," *Alon Shevut* 108 (5748), 9]

Fraternal Hatred

When the eternal character of the Jewish collective was at stake, it was clear to Yosef that even with all the distress he was causing his father, he was operating as his agent. He therefore arranged that the brothers would once again face the same situation, only this time with Binyamin. They again had to face the possibility of hurting their father – "For how can I go back to my father unless the boy is with me? Let me not witness the woe that would overtake my father!" (*Bereshit* 44:34). The internalization of this message, that fraternal hatred damages the Jewish collective in its entirety, constitutes a critical prerequisite for the establishment of the character of the nation. Clearly, this eternal lesson could not prevent occasional flare-ups of hatred throughout our history, but at every such moment this warning accompanies us like a torch, a torch with the capability to illuminate our history, to guide and enlighten, but also, God forbid, to burn and destroy. ["The Ramifications of Fraternal Strife," Shabbat *Parashat Vayigash*, 5759]

Frumkeit

[We are now witnessing] other phenomena never seen before in the Religious Zionist community. Young men wear large knitted *kippot*, long sidelocks, sockless sandals and untucked shirts – true "*Chasidim*." It is as if they are proclaiming, "I am religious. Even if my *kippa* flies off in the wind, my long sidelocks will pull me and bind me to the religious camp." Long sidelocks and *tzitzit* that dangle at one's knees have no halakhic-religious meaning; however, they grant one a certain sense of security and express a certain type of fervent religiosity and ultra-orthodoxy. I hear of *Yeshivot Hesder* where the students don *tefillin* for *Mincha* prayers. *Tefillin* add holiness. Halakhically, this practice is not arrogant or otherwise inappropriate; in fact, technically, the opposite is true. But I belong to a different generation. I have been fortunate enough to pray with some of our *Gedolim*: Rav Shlomo Zalman Auerbach, Rav Yitzchak Weiss (author of *Minchat Yitzchak*), Rav Isser Zalman Melzer and Rav Aharon Kotler, and I never saw any of them recite *Mincha* wearing *tefillin*. No one in the previous generation would have considered wearing *tefillin* for *Mincha* when the *Gedolim* did not, despite what the technical *halakha* may suggest. Thirty years ago, I was told by Rabbi Bergman, the son-in-law of Rav Schach and a close disciple of the Chazon Ish, that he once decided to build a *sukka* according to all the specifications of the Chazon Ish: a *sukka* without any nails. On the eve of *Sukkot*, he suddenly thought, "How can I have a '*mehudar*' *sukka* when my grandfather did not?" He immediately took some nails and fastened them into his *sukka*. ["Religious Insecurity and its Cures," *Alei Etzion* 15 (5767), 10]

༄

Our generation has lost faith in its predecessors and feels the need to "start from scratch." Suddenly, all kinds of new customs are being rediscovered in the *Mishna Berura*. Religious behavior of this kind has its drawbacks; stringencies can be a sign of weakness. A student of mine who teaches in one of the *yeshivot Hesder* recently told me, "When I see students who wear *tefillin* for *Mincha*, I know that there are other students who skip *Mincha* entirely." ["Religious Insecurity and its Cures," *Alei Etzion* 15 (5767), 10]

༄

In Yiddish, the term *"frumkeit"* is generally associated with a sense of heaviness and an overly fastidious observance of the *mitzvot*. In both the Chasidic and *Musar* movements, there were those who saw in *frumkeit* an important value; others dissociated themselves entirely from it, as in Slobodka and in Kotzk. The negative aspects of *frumkeit* generally include a greater emphasis placed on "turning away from evil" than on "doing good" (cf. *Tehillim* 34:15) and a strictness that is applied primarily to others. The fear of sin occasionally leads to a certain passivity – a fear of taking action – which leads to a freezing of the creative process and an avoidance of all struggle. Thus, so-called "fear of God" can lead to self-nullification, which can in turn lead to total inactivity. My grandmother, *Hy"d*, was a very righteous woman with simple faith. I remember waking up every morning and finding my shoes polished. My grandmother told me that since I spent my days studying Torah, the least she could do was polish my shoes. This notwithstanding, she would often quote the popular saying that *"frum"* is an acronym for *"fiel rishus veinig mitzvos"* ("much wickedness and few *mitzvot*"). [*Jewish Values*, 15-16]

∽∘∾

The importance of tension in life notwithstanding, a person must guard himself against excessive tension and anxiety in his worship of God. Just as in every other realm of life, exaggeration is seen as abnormal, so too in the observance of *mitzvot*. This stands in contrast to the prevalent view that equates excessive meticulousness with fear of Heaven. Rambam, in his *Shemona Perakim* (Chapter 4), notes that a person should strive to reach the level at which he can easily follow the golden mean in all his character traits, instead of constantly struggling with his baser inclinations. Excessive anxiety and suspicion are liable to lead to total paralysis. Here, too, a person must find the proper balance. [*Jewish Values*, 113]

Government

Has it ever before happened in Jewish history that a *Rosh Yeshiva* was called upon to join a government? The sense that we are experiencing a great historical moment causes me to think that there are far wider implications than we may now realize. Yesterday, I was at the home of the President for a photograph session together with all the other ministers. A journalist asked me: "Are you excited?" I told him: "I forgot to be excited." When my eldest son was born, I went to my wife's grandfather, Rav Isser Zalman Meltzer, *zt"l*, to tell him the news. He wished me "*Mazal tov*," but after a few minutes he turned to me and said: "I must apologize to you. I am sure you can see that I am not as happy as a grandfather should be upon the birth of a grandchild, but ever since the Holocaust I have lost the ability to rejoice in family celebrations." I was reminded of this story and of something that my teacher Rav Ya'akov Moshe Charlap, *zt"l*, wrote: "When King David thanks God for His kindness, David refers to himself in the third person (II *Shemuel* 22:51): 'He does kindness to His anointed, to David and his seed forever.' He does not speak of himself in the first person because he is so intensely possessed of the feeling of *shelichut*, of being a messenger of the people. There was no room left for any personal individual feeling. The idea, not the individual, is central." Although I cannot claim, like King David, to have no personal feeling, my sense of my individual role has decreased greatly. In light of what we have recently experienced [the assassination of the Prime Minister], I feel that it is not me being discussed, but a mission, a rescue; therefore, I was not excited by becoming a minister. ["Speech upon Harav Amital's Appointment as a Minister in the Government," *Alei Etzion* 5 (5756), 9-10]

∽∾

The problem of acceptance of governmental authority – "'You shall surely appoint a king over you' (*Devarim* 17:15) – so that the fear of him will be upon you" (*Ketubot* 17a) – always existed in *Am Yisrael*. It is for this reason that Halakha is strict in this regard and rules that a person who rebels against the sovereign is liable to the death penalty (*Tosefta*, *Terumot* 7:20). The problem is especially grave in our times, with extremists on the left and the right who are not prepared to accept the sovereign authority. This is the first time that an organized, religious, nationalist and Zionist group has decided that it does not accept the authority of the sovereign State of Israel. Sovereignty is thereby weakened. In principle, I would agree that there are times when it is necessary to rebel, but it must be borne in mind that the problem of not accepting authority – rebellion against the sovereign power – is one of the most difficult questions in Halakha; it is certainly no less grave than the matter of freeing a woman whose husband will not grant her a divorce. It is therefore unacceptable that every first-year yeshiva student can rule when it is permissible to reject the authority of the sovereign power. Sometimes people think that through their actions they are strengthening *Eretz Yisrael*, but they do not pay attention to the fact that at the same time they are weakening the sovereignty in *Eretz Yisrael*. ["This is the Day that God Has

Made; We Shall Be Happy and Rejoice in It,'" *Alon Shevut Bogrim* 3 (5754), 96]

                        ⱷⱷ

We must put a stop to the delegitimization of a government that was democratically elected. A Jewish majority decided that a Knesset majority is fit and authorized to make decisions. Recognition of the authority of the Knesset and the government stood at the foundation of the entire religious Zionist partnership in the State, and from this arose its active participation in the leadership of the State and its institutions. An undermining of this authority may lead to absolute anarchy and a collapse of the institutions of law and order. With this in mind, we must stop talking about civil insurrection, since the distance between that and violent insurrection is not all that great. ["Soulsearching," *Alon Shevut Bogrim* 8 (5756), 13]

                        ⱷⱷ

We must remember that throughout the generations, respect was shown towards the leaders of the nation even where they did not behave in accordance with the way of the Torah. David called Sha'ul "the anointed one of God" (I *Shemuel* 24:6) even after Sha'ul wiped out Nov, the city of *kohanim*, and violated God's command. At the beginning of *Hilkhot Chanukka* (3:1), the Rambam explains the importance of the festival as commemorating the fact that "Israelite sovereignty (*malkhut*) returned for more than two hundred years;" he uses the term "*malkhut*" in relation to the Hasmonean kings, despite the offensive behavior of many of them. The *Kohen Gadol* would pray on Yom Kippur

(*Hilkhot Avodat Yom ha-Kippurim* 3:11) that "God should deliver Israel and not leave them without their king." One may disagree with the path; one may demonstrate and protest, but one must continue to show respect towards the elected government of Israel, as practiced by religious Zionism since its inception. ["Soulsearching," *Alon Shevut Bogrim* 8 (5756), 14]

∾o∾

This line of thought that demonizes the government is likely to cause a most profound educational crisis. Throughout the years we believed in the Hand of God guiding events, as we have seen with our own eyes in the return to Zion in our generation. By God's mercy, I have merited to witness the establishment of the State and its building, its withstanding all of the Arab nations, its extraordinary development, within a few decades, into a country with military, political and economic power. Having seen all this, I cannot understand the murmurings in our camp about "the imminent end of the State," "destruction," etc. Such talk evidences weak faith. ["Soulsearching," *Alon Shevut Bogrim* 8 (5756), 14]

Halakha

We live in an era in which educated religious circles like to emphasize the centrality of Halakha, and commitment to it, in Judaism. I can say that in my youth in pre-Holocaust Hungary, I didn't hear people talking all the time about "Halakha." People conducted themselves in the tradition of their forefathers, and where any halakhic problem arose, they consulted a rabbi. Reliance on Halakha and unconditional commitment to it mean, for many people, a stable anchor whose purpose is to maintain the purity of Judaism, even within the modern world. To my mind, this excessive emphasis of Halakha has exacted a high cost. The impression created is that there is nothing in Torah but that which exists in Halakha, and that in any confrontation with the new problems that arise in modern society, answers should be sought exclusively in books of Halakha. Many of the fundamental values of the Torah which are based on the general commandments of "You shall be holy" (*Vayikra* 19:2) and "You shall do what is upright and good in the eyes of God" (*Devarim* 6:18), which were not given formal, operative formulation, have not only lost some of their status, but they have also lost their validity in the eyes of a public that regards itself as committed to Halakha. ["Not Everything is Halakha," *Alon Shevut Bogrim* 13 (5759), 96]

∽○∽

A Jew must aspire to mold himself in such a way as to become more genuine, more moral. Otherwise, he will turn into a "scoundrel within the bounds of Torah" (Ramban, *Vayikra* 19:2). The Torah talks about a "wayward and rebellious son" (*Devarim* 21:18) who is punctilious in his observance of the minutest laws of keeping kosher (*Sanhedrin* 8:2). It is specifically he, says the Torah – that same person who is so careful about kosher symbols – who can turn into a "scoundrel within the bounds of the Torah." ["Approaching Elul," *Alon Shevut Bogrim* 4 (5755), 38]

౪౦౪

Whereas Halakha may be simple, the evaluation of reality is complex. Just as Judaism rejects the Karaite negation of the Oral Law, maintaining instead that there is no Written Law without the interpretation of the Oral Law, so we must also reject a "Karaite" approach to Halakha. Halakha that is devoid of the exegesis of reality is a sort of Karaite law. This "Karaite" approach has led to Halakha as a whole becoming, for the youth, something autistic, unconnected with reality… This, among other factors, also unquestionably influences the claims that are being voiced today by youth in the religious education system: "The Torah doesn't connect with us;" "The Torah isn't something that relates to reality;" "The Torah isn't our 'thing.'" ["Not Everything is Halakha," *Alon Shevut Bogrim* 13 (5759), 97-98]

౪౦౪

We must put a stop to the superficial invocation of Halakha in political matters. Halakha can be a dangerous explosive when it is placed in the hands of the youth instead of being decided by great Torah scholars. Halakha as a concept is too broad and too holy to be left to the discretion of young people who lack the breadth of knowledge that is necessary for a Torah decision in such matters. ["Soulsearching," *Alon Shevut Bogrim* 8 (5756), 12]

❧

The halakhic arguments offered by certain rabbis are generally based on a reading of the political map in accordance with right-wing political views on matters surrounded by public controversy, such as the issue of the dangers and possibilities of the peace process. These arguments are based on a selective interpretation and preference for opinions of certain *Rishonim* and contemporary authorities – such as a preference for the approach of the Ramban concerning the commandment to conquer the land (whose relevance in our times is itself subject to debate among the major authorities) over the approach of the Rambam and other *Rishonim*, and a preference for rulings by rabbis from a certain circle over the rulings of rabbis from other circles. For some reason, these preferences always correlate with the political views of those rabbis. We are not speaking here of abstract ideological positions, but rather of practical halakhic rulings in existential questions with life-and-death ramifications. ["Soulsearching," *Alon Shevut Bogrim* 8 (5756), 12]

❧

In matters of public, state policy, the Torah does not set down any unequivocal law that will automatically be relevant to any situation and to every generation. When it comes to fateful questions, the national leadership must take into consideration a whole collection of factors – spiritual, security-related, social and economic. Can we possi-

Halakha

bly speak of unequivocal "Halakha" that can provide a uniform answer to every situation, at every time, without taking into consideration all of those factors? ["Soulsearching," *Alon Shevut Bogrim* 8 (5756), 13]

∽∾

One of the fundamental tenets of Judaism is that our Torah is a Torah of life, always addressing concrete reality. Torah can never arrive at a head-on collision with reality, such that the important needs of life are harmed. ["Not Everything is Halakha," *Alon Shevut Bogrim* 13 (5759), 97]

Happiness

A person can develop only if he is happy. Without *joie de vivre*, in a situation of depression, one cannot develop. We do not demand of every individual to behave in accordance with such heavy demands as exemplified, for example, by Rabbeinu Yona or *Mesillat Yesharim*. We do not make extravagant demands in connection with "You shall love your neighbor as yourself" (*Vayikra* 19:18). All in all, we are required to be human beings – not to wallow in bitterness, not to go about with a sour face, but rather to go about with a smile. ["Parting Speech," *Daf Kesher* 18 (5746)]

Hearing the Baby's Cry

When the first group of students came to the yeshiva, they asked me: "What's special about this yeshiva?" I told them the Chasidic story about *Ba'al ha-Tanya*, who was sitting and studying in the inner room of the house. His grandson, the *Tzemach Tzedek*, sat in the middle room. In the outer room there was a baby in a cradle. The baby suddenly awoke from his sleep and began to cry. The *Tzemach Tzedek* was so immersed in his study that he did not hear the baby crying, but the *Ba'al ha-Tanya*, whose room was further away, did hear. He stopped learning and emerged from the room to calm the baby. On his way back, he passed the room where the *Tzemach Tzedek* sat and told him: "When a person studies Torah and does not hear a cry for help, something is deficient in his learning." ["Hearing the Baby's Cry," *Alon Shevut Bogrim* 1 (5754), 83]

༄

When Rav Ya'aqov Medan came to me and told me that he was going to embark on a hunger strike [to protest the handover of weapons to the Palestinian Authority at the time of the Oslo Accords], I said to him: "Reb Ya'aqov, you know that I am fundamentally opposed to hunger strikes. I also read the political map differently from the way you do. But I cannot hide the fact that I am proud. The yeshiva's first student is fulfilling its educational message: when a Jewish child is crying, he closes his Gemara and takes care of the crying of the baby." ["Hearing the Baby's Cry," *Alon Shevut Bogrim* 1 (5754), 83]

కాం

Some words speak; others send a message. There are times when words denote nothing more than their plain sense; but there are also times when words send out a message that tells us much more than what was actually stated. A person must be sensitive enough to hear what lies behind the words. I often tell the Chasidic tale about Rav Moshe of Kobrin, who every now and then would visit rabbis and *tzaddikim* in order to see how they served God. Rav Moshe arrived one Friday afternoon in the town of Rav Yisrael of Apta, and he went to see how Rav Yisrael would prepare himself for Shabbat. When everything was ready, Rav Yisrael went into the *beit midrash* and began to read aloud *Shir ha-Shirim* with great concentration and intensity. Rav Moshe was beside himself with elation, greatly impressed by what he saw. All of a sudden, the door opened, and a barnyard stench permeated the *beit midrash*. A Jewish cowherd approached Rav Yisrael and cried out: "Rebbe, my cow, my cow!" Rav Yisrael interrupted his reading of *Shir ha-Shirim*, and asked what was wrong. The cowherd explained that his cow, which was ready to calve, was experiencing difficulties in the birthing process, and were the cow to die, he would lose his livelihood, God forbid. The Rebbe calmed him down, sent him to a veterinarian, and even gave the cow a blessing of health. Rav Moshe of Kobrin, who witnessed the entire incident, was very troubled by what he had seen. Simple-minded Jews must be brought near to religion, but Rabbi Akiva teaches (*Yadayim* 3:5), "while all books of the Bible are holy, *Shir ha-Shirim* is holy of holies!" How could Rav Yisrael interrupt his recitation of *Shir ha-Shirim* for a cow? Rav Moshe waited until after the Shabbat meal and then asked: "Is there no limit to the degree to which one must relate to simple-minded Jews?" The Rebbe answered him: "Did you hear the Jew's cry?" "Certainly," responded Rav Moshe, "he cried out, 'My cow, my cow!'" The Rebbe said to him: "You weren't listening well. The Jew was crying: 'Rebbe, I am nothing; please draw me close to you!'" This may not have been what the cowherd said, but this is the message he conveyed. The simple Jew sought the Rebbe's closeness, but what could he talk to him about? The only possibility he had of creating a connection with the Rebbe was by way of his everyday needs. His words sent out a message that went far beyond what was actually stated. [*Jewish Values*, 167-168]

Historical Perspective

Someone who does not understand the meaning of an entire nation being exiled from its land cannot understand the historical significance of its return. *Eretz Yisrael* was entirely emptied of all her inhabitants. Has such a thing ever happened in history – a nation that was exiled from its land, and returns to it?

The prophet says, "Old men and old women shall yet again dwell in the streets of Jerusalem, and every man with his staff in his hand because of his old age; and the streets of the city shall be full of boys and girls playing in its streets" (*Zekharia* 8:4-5). This describes simple, normal life. Only someone with a deep historical awareness can understand the significance of such a scene. Miracles are one-time events. But Jews living a normal life in *Eretz Yisrael* after seventy years (of the Babylonian exile) during which the country was empty and desolate – someone looking with historical perspective can only be astonished. Of him the prophet says, "If it will be wondrous in the eyes of the remnant of this nation in those days, it will also be wondrous in My eyes, says the Lord of hosts" (8:6).

Normal life, that which other nations accept as a natural phenomenon, is perceived by us as a meta-historical one, a manifestation of the Divine. For them everything is "smooth" – "I gave unto Esav Mount Seir, to possess it" (*Yehoshua* 24:4); such is the way of the world. But "Yaakov and his sons went down to Egypt" (*ibid.*). For us, every natural phenomenon becomes a supernatural one. For us, everything is always different.

After two thousand years, children play in the streets of Israel, and old people sit in the squares of Jerusalem! Can this be a natural phenomenon, after two thousand years? For us, everything is always different. ["This is the Day that God Has Made; We Shall Be Happy and Rejoice in It," *Alon Shevut Bogrim* 3 (5754), 92]

∽o∾

Someone who lacks a historical awareness, someone who sees only the present and is cut off from the past, is incapable of seeing the future, and perceives even the present in a distorted way. ["This is the Day that God Has Made; We Shall Be Happy and Rejoice in It," *Alon Shevut Bogrim* 3 (5754), 92]

∽o∾

Today we live in a "now" generation: Peace now, Mashiach now, Terrorism now, Quiet now; everything must be now. We are incapable of imagining what tomorrow might bring. Everything is measured by the yardstick of what is happening today. Today is quiet – tomorrow will be too. Today there is terrorism – tomorrow it will continue. Today there is peace – tomorrow there will be peace. It is a generation with an impaired sense of history… Someone who cannot see the past will also be incapable of seeing the future, and of perceiving God's hand, "when God redeems the captivity of His nation" (*Tehillim* 126:1). Can a nation rising out of the ashes of the *Shoah* allow itself to ignore this? ["This is the Day that God Has Made; We Shall Be Happy and Rejoice in It," *Alon Shevut Bogrim* 3 (5754), 94]

∾o∾

I am thankful to the Holy One, Blessed be He, for each and every moment, for each and every breath, for giving me strength. Once they used to say that thirty years was a "generation." Today, they're talking about ten years, or even less. There are such great changes. I don't believe that old people always have an opinion to contribute, but sometimes they have something to contribute out of their life experience. However, I do not regard myself as someone who belongs to the "old" generation. ["Understand the Years of Each Generation," *Alon Shevut Bogrim* 13 (5759), 141]

Holocaust

When my mother suggested that I take a picture of the family with me, I refused. I told her that I had no need of such memories, that we would meet again. I could not allow myself to give expression to the feeling that I had no hope of ever seeing my parents alive again. I did not want to give my parents any hint that such thoughts resided within me. [*A World Built*, 133]

❧

At the end of the war, I managed to travel from Hungary to Bucharest, and from there I had an opportunity of getting to Israel. The caravan was planning to leave on Shabbat. An argument broke out among us as to whether we were allowed to desecrate Shabbat in order to join the caravan. I argued vigorously that to begin our journey was a matter of life and death, and thus it was permitted. I could not help remembering that only a few weeks beforehand, a Russian soldier had placed a loaded gun next to my heart. [*A World Built*, 134]

❧

I was in a Nazi labor camp, and I remember one day – it was the day after Yom Kippur – that I had nothing to eat. I searched for food together with my cousin, and we found a piece of moldy bread, a few days old. That was enough for me. For many years after that, when I would sit down to eat and see sliced bread on the table, I would think about how many Jews one could feed with those slices. ["You Loved Us and You Desired Us?" *Alon Shevut Bogrim* 18 (5763), 95]

∽∽∾

During the past forty years, I have often recalled the horrors that I lived through. Millions of Jews were murdered in the Holocaust – yet I was saved. Was I saved because God singled me out and made sure that I would not suffer the same fate as millions of others of our people? Or was it merely a matter of chance? The verse states, "And I will surely hide My face on that day" (*Devarim* 31:18). When God hides His countenance from us, it is because, as the verse tells us, "And if you walk contrary to Me… then will I also walk contrary to you" (*Vayikra* 26:23–24). The Ramban explains that God, in effect, tells us, "I will leave you in the hands of chance" (Commentary on *Iyyov* 36:7). Perhaps God had decided to leave His people in the hands of chance and, as a part of a fortunate accident, I was saved. If such is the case, then my salvation was a result of God acting in a contrary manner towards His people, and not because He saw fit to single me out among millions. If I positively knew that the Holy One, Blessed be He, chose me, that God had singled me out for some special purpose, then such knowledge would, indeed, place a great burden upon me. I doubt that I would have been able to live up to and achieve what was expected of me. Yet, I would gladly relinquish all the wealth and riches of the world, if it were true that God had chosen to bestow His grace upon me, as an individual among millions. These doubts plague me to this day. Clearly, the answer lies in the hands of God, and because I do not know the answer, I do not have the boldness to designate a specific day as a holiday because I was saved. [*A World Built*, 134-135]

∽o∾

I am a simple person. Nevertheless, I sensed that I had to garner all the power within me, doubling and redoubling it, in order to recompense for those who are no longer with us. This knowledge gave me the daring and courage to accomplish things that were far beyond my normal abilities. [*A World Built*, 135]

∽o∾

To our great distress, we are witness today to the widespread suppression of the Holocaust from our religious consciousness. Admittedly, it is difficult to deal with the *Shoah*. One of the ways of dealing with it, which certain people have employed, is simply removing it from our minds, ignoring it – not in the historical sense, but in the religious and spiritual sense. I am not speaking of the pernicious phenomenon of Holocaust denial, which maintains that the *Shoah* never happened. Rather, I refer to the absenting of the *Shoah* from the public memory and from our religious awareness, whether consciously or unconsciously – particularly here in Israel. When people use loaded words like "Auschwitz," "Majdanek," "Nazis," etc., to describe other phenomena – serious though they may be – that is a belittling of the *Shoah*. Using terms derived from the *Shoah* to describe acts of terrorism will cause future generations to come to a point where only the historians among them will be able to differentiate between the Holocaust and Israel's wars. The carelessness of such speech is bound to bring us to a future where the term *"Shoah"* itself will come to be a general term for a disaster to the Jewish people, and perhaps "World War II" will be a synonym for the German destruction of our people. When Jews use terms borrowed from the world of Holocaust images against other Jews, they too belittle the *Shoah*. Whether it is leftists calling Israeli soldiers "Judeo-Nazis," or rightists shouting "S.S." and "Gestapo" at Israeli police officers, both belittle the *Shoah*, even if the ultimate intent of their protests is good and their aim is for the sake of Heaven. [*A World Built*, 142-43]

∽∘∾

In 1996, I was asked to participate in a panel discussion. At one point, one of the participants asked me: "Is it still possible to refer to the State of Israel as 'the dawn of our redemption' now, after four cities were given over to the Palestinians as part of the Oslo Accords?" Immediately, a rabbi, one of the leaders of the religious Zionist camp, stood up and replied, "It is an *a fortiori* argument: if, seventy years ago, Rabbi Kook in his correspondence could refer to the embryonic State of Israel as 'the dawn of our redemption,' certainly we can, all the more so, do likewise today!" Yet, in my mind, a question remained: "All the more so"? Is that really true? Was not our world destroyed in the intervening seventy years? Did the most terrifying event not happen in the meantime? This approach, found among some members of the religious Zionist community, also ignores the *Shoah*, springing from a personal inability to deal with it. [*A World Built*, 144-45]

∽∘∾

We stand silent before the enormity of the *Shoah*, and we have no answer. "And Your faithfulness in the nights" (*Tehillim* 92:3) – even when it is darkest, we believe that God is faithful to us. This is one of the tests with which God tries us. Despite everything, we continue to cling to God, echoing the ironic lament: "We fled from You – to You." But as for a reply, there is none. [*A World Built*, 143]

౭౦౬

Shortly after I arrived in *Eretz Yisrael*, I visited Kfar Etzion and chanced upon a friend whom I had known during those dark days. When he saw me, he cried out, "Yehuda – is it you? You were saved? You, who always preached to us that we have no hope and should prepare to die as martyrs sanctifying God's Name – you were saved!?" His next question was: "Did you remain religious?" I replied, "Had I not stayed religious, would all of the questions have been answered? Would the whole phenomenon then be understandable?" [*A World Built*, 149]

౭౦౬

I clearly experienced the hand of God during the Holocaust – only I did not understand its meaning. It was so clear – so abnormal, so unnatural, so illogical. I was not in Auschwitz, but I saw Jews being taken there. I saw regiments of Germans who were not going to the Russian front, but rather guarding the trainloads of Jews that were headed to the death camps. It went against all military logic and interests. Can one possibly begin to understand such madness? I saw the hand of God in everything. It was not natural; it was not human. I saw the hand of God, but I did not understand its significance. [*A World Built*, 138-39]

❧

The Holocaust has become deeply ingrained within the consciousness of our people, even if we are not always aware of its influence upon us. I see the influence of the Holocaust in everything that has occurred since then: in the flight that many have taken from Judaism and in the return that many are embarking upon in search of their Jewish heritage and roots; in extremism; in Kahanism; and in Peace Now. I believe and hope that there is a possibility for inner change. The trials and tribulations of our people refine us, and even though many of our experiences seem to have a negative and adverse effect upon us, our nation is becoming better. The time will soon come when we will reveal the inner beauty of the entire nation of Israel. [*A World Built*, 139]

❧

There is nothing in the world that can justify the death of hundreds of thousands of children, who were killed and burned. Nothing in the world can justify that! Not the State of Israel, not the coming of the Messiah, not the Jewish People repenting. Nothing in the world can justify it! ["You Loved Us and You Desired Us?" *Alon Shevut Bogrim* 18 (5763), 96]

❧

Some people speak about the "hiding of God's face" (*Devarim* 31:17, *Chagiga* 5a). What does it mean that He "hides His face"? Is God a person, who can hide his face and not see? We cry out in bewilderment, together with the prophet Chavakkuk (1:13): "Your eyes are too pure to see evil; You cannot look upon iniquity. Why do You look upon those who deal treacherously and remain silent while the wicked man devours one who is more righteous than he?" ["You Loved Us and You Desired Us?" *Alon Shevut Bogrim* 18 (5763), 97]

∽∘∾

During those terrible days it was difficult for me to say (in the middle blessing of the Festival prayers), "You loved us and You desired us" – but I said it, and I continue to say it. It would seem that the time has come, in view of the millions of Jews who continue to say, "You loved us and You desired us," for the Holy One, Blessed be He, to love us and desire us. "You will arise and have mercy upon Zion, for the time has come…" (*Tehillim* 102:14). ["You Loved Us and You Desired Us?" *Alon Shevut Bogrim* 18 (5763), 98]

Honesty

The Ramban, in disagreement with the Rambam in this regard, maintains that prayer is a mitzva of rabbinic origin. He writes (Glosses to *Sefer ha-Mitzvot, Aseh* 5): "The essence of the verse (*Devarim* 11:13), 'And to serve Him with all your heart,' is a positive commandment that all of our service of God, may He be Blessed, should be with our entire heart, that is to say, with perfect, desirable intention, directed to His Name, and without evil thoughts. We should not perform the *mitzvot* without intention or based on the uncertain premise that perhaps they will lead to some benefit." In other words, according to the Ramban, there is a separate mitzva that a person should have full spiritual backing for his performance of the *mitzvot*. Thus, simplicity and wholeness are also values in mitzva observance; there should be no difference between a person's service of God in the privacy of his own home and his worship in the public arena. These are connected to the trait of modesty, for a person whose outward behavior does not match his conduct at home suffers from the flaw of external pride. There is a famous saying that it is lucky for the Jews that the mitzva of *lulav* and *etrog* (taking the Four Species on Sukkot) is fulfilled in public, whereas the mitzva of *maror* (eating bitter herbs at the Seder) is fulfilled in the privacy of a person's home. Were the opposite true, then many people would be less fastidious about their *lulav* and *etrog*, and instead they would make special efforts to fulfill the mitzva of *maror* in the best possible manner. [*Jewish Values*, 88-90]

∽◦∾

It is imperative that our conduct be truthful, without pos-turing or putting on shows. This is especially important regarding the ability of parents and teachers to exert edu-cational influence. Children do not always know how to express their criticism, but they can almost always sense whether their parents are speaking honestly to them or just putting on a show. One of the main problems in education is that parents demand from their children norms of behav-ior that they themselves do not live up to. Authenticity has enormous power and is likely to have great educational impact. [*Jewish Values*, 92]

Humanity

The worship of God, in whatever form, cannot wipe out simple human feeling. The Rebbe of Kotzk would say about the verse: "And you shall be holy people to Me" (*Shemot* 22:30), that God, as it were, is saying here: "Angels I have in sufficient quantity; I am looking for *human beings* who will be holy *people*." [*Jewish Values*, 193]

૭๐๛

There has been a tendency in recent years to idealize great rabbis, to the point of total disregard of their human feelings and weaknesses. The Torah presents the opposite approach: every person has a human side, which must not be denied. Even the prophets had doubts and difficulties. The Torah recognizes that man lives in this world, and it has no expectation that one behave as if he were living in an ideal and unreal universe. [*Jewish Values*, 195]

૭๐๛

A person who reads the story of the *Akeda* (Binding) of Yitzchak (*Bereshit* 22) superficially thinks that it portrays only the acceptance of God's command in silence and submission. Avraham is commanded to slaughter his son, and out of his recognition that nothing stands in the way of God's command, he nullifies his will before the will of the Holy One, Blessed be He. All at once, everything else is set aside; everything is nullified. There is no paternal love for his son, no mercy, no human sensitivity, no considerations of morality. Everything is silenced, dissolved; it disappears in the face of the Divine command. To my mind, such a view is completely mistaken. I believe that the father's love for his son did not disappear, nor did it dissolve. Quite the opposite: its power was a prerequisite for the entire *Akeda*. ["Grace and Mercy and Compassion," *Alon Shevut Bogrim* 15 (5762), 9]

Independence

A person is further expected to be capable of deciding issues on his own. His character is also measured according to his decision-making ability. There are those who believe that, ideally, a person should turn to a rabbi for guidance in all matters; they see this as an elevated expression of fear of Heaven. In my opinion, this is a problematic phenomenon, one that contradicts what is expected of man. It also runs counter to our prayer, in the second blessing after the evening recitation of the *Shema*, "And instill within us good counsel from before You." Rabbi Schneur Zalman of Liadi, the *Baal ha-Tanya*, writes (*Iggeret ha-Kodesh* 22): "My beloved, my brethren and friends: Out of [my] hidden love [for you, springs] an overt rebuke. 'Come now and let us debate' (*Yeshayahu* 1:18); 'remember the days of old, consider the years of every generation' (*Devarim* 32:7). Has such a thing ever happened in days past? Where indeed have you found such a custom in any of the books of the early or latter sages of Israel, that it should be the custom and established norm to ask for advice in mundane matters, as to what one ought to do in matters of the physical world?" [*Jewish Values*, 218]

Individual and Community

Modern Western society revolves around three central values, all of which relate to the individual: individual rights, individual liberty and individual privacy. It appears at times as though these have attained the status of absolute values which may not be violated under any circumstances. Their effect on society and culture is discernible in almost every sphere, from legislation, through education, literature and art to the prevailing everyday lifestyle.

"Privacy of the individual" occupies a special place, for it is the most comprehensive and the attitude towards it borders on worship. Based on this value, a number of rules have been established which leave their mark on all social relationships. For example, any conversation between two people who are not members of the same family or close friends must be pragmatic and to-the-point, free of anything personal. Any personal comment or question, or even a show of interest in the personal condition or feelings of one's partner in conversation, is regarded as rude, a desecration of the holy value of privacy and a vulgar violation of his private life. Every person is a closed world, and no one else has the right to penetrate it. As a result, there is a growing sense of alienation in Western society in general, and in the United States in particular. There is "I" and there is "he," but there is almost never a "we." ["From Commitment to Responsibility," *Alei Etzion* 12 (5764), 7-8]

Insubordination

The halakhic ruling published by religious Zionist rabbis, according to which a soldier must refuse orders during the evacuation of IDF bases in Yehuda and Shomron (the West Bank), gives rise to a range of thoughts. On the halakhic level, the ruling has no basis whatsoever. At most, we might define a soldier who participates in the physical evacuation of a base as indirectly assisting in a forbidden act (assuming that some transgression is indeed involved). Clearly, even without the assistance of those soldiers who might obey the ruling and refuse orders, it will still be possible to evacuate the bases. For this reason, we are clearly not talking about a biblical prohibition, and it is most doubtful whether there is even a rabbinical prohibition involved. Clearly, it is a ruling with far-reaching ramifications. One of the most important elements of the religious Zionist view has always been participation in the Israel Defense Forces. This is a blood pact that has proved itself in all of Israel's wars. There is no need to elaborate on the damage that would be caused to this value of the unity of the nation and the army as a result of a mass refusal of orders. Does this huge damage not take precedence over a situation of a great doubt as to a rabbinical prohibition? Had the call remained within the confines of a socio-political declaration, as an act of protest or the like, we could discuss it on these levels, but the halakhic stamp of approval awarded to this call seems baseless. ["A Political Opinion in Halakhic Garb," *Meimad* 5 (5757), 7]

∽o∾

The ruling of the rabbis who called upon IDF soldiers to refuse orders asserts that dismantling the military bases creates a situation of *pikuach nefesh* (danger to human life). We must consider who holds the authority to assert that this is actually the situation. Just as in medical matters one must consult doctors, who are assumed to possess professional expertise, so too in matters of security the authority to define a situation as a security danger rests with the government of Israel and the heads of the army, just as we recognize their authority when it comes to going to war and other security-related activities. Therefore, anyone who is guided by the values of religious Zionism and the unity of the nation bears the responsibility for preventing a rift in the nation and for weighing his steps carefully, with a broad view of the world of Halakha. In particular he must beware of dressing political views in halakhic garb, which involves misleading a public that stands perplexed in the face of such a ruling. ["A Political Opinion in Halakhic Garb," *Meimad* 5 (5757), 7]

Jewish Identity

Jewish society as a whole is in the midst of a process of losing its Jewish identity. If this process continues, God forbid, it represents a real existential danger to the State of Israel. On the one hand, we already have hundreds of thousands of Jews who have immigrated in recent years from the countries of Eastern Europe and have no knowledge at all of Jewish history. They are Jews who have no concept of Judaism, who have never heard of our nation's heroes, who are devoid of any sense of Jewish pride. On the other hand, there are the youth of today, in schools and institutions of higher education, whose knowledge of Judaism is close to that of their brethren who have immigrated from the former Soviet Union. Religious Judaism has erred in thinking that it could cope with this issue alone. It made two mistakes. The first was to let the secular public off the hook with regard to dealing with this problem. It transmitted the message, both consciously and unconsciously, that dealing with the problem is the job of religious Judaism; it did not cooperate with the non-religious public to a sufficient degree. A further mistake was to present the matter as a religious problem and not as a national Jewish problem. This led to the antagonism that we see today. And we stand and wonder: is it possible that there still exists in Israel that innocent faith that maintains that being born in Israel and speaking Hebrew will suffice for a person to be bound, heart and soul, to the State of Israel and the Jewish nation?

["The Nation Grows Mighty While Its Discourse Grows Weak," *Ammudim* 563 (5753), 205]

❦

Unfortunately, a great many schools in Israel are raising rootless youth, youth who are cut off from any connection with Judaism. I regard this as an existential danger to the State of Israel. The spiritual destitution in the realm of Judaism is reaching terrifying proportions. Not only is the language of the *Tanakh* and the stories of our Sages unintelligible, even the language of [Nobel laureate S.Y.] Agnon and the finest of our modern authors is unintelligible to the youth growing up today in Israel. To paraphrase a poem by Rabbi Yehuda Ha-Levi, who once declared that "the nation grows weak while its discourse grows mighty," we may state that in Israel today the nation grows mighty while its discourse grows weak. ["The Nation Grows Mighty While Its Discourse Grows Weak," *Ammudim* 563 (5753), 205]

❦

The great majority of the nation is still connected to our tradition. There are two groups that are dangerous. One is actively dangerous, while the other presents a passive danger. The active group is made up of people, mostly intellectuals, who are not interested in Jewish identity. The second group is made up of Russian immigrants who know nothing about Judaism. The problem is that the first group stands at the center of influence in the media and in the decision-making hierarchy. This should not concern rabbis alone. Every Jew should make an effort to save the country. A country without Jewish identity will not be able to survive. Today there is abhorrence for religious coercion, but the nation – for the most part – is still open to tradition, on different levels. ["Hearing the Baby's Cry," *Alon Shevut Bogrim* 1 (5754), 87]

Kahanism

The creation of a religious nationalist ideology with an extreme political stance, against the backdrop of the hundred-year-long, blood-drenched Arab-Israeli conflict, led to an undermining of fundamental principles. The centrality of personal and national morality, and of the sanctity of human life, were pushed aside in favor of aggression, hatred, nationalism, and racism. The Kahanist group, more than any other, symbolized the dangerous, malignant growth of the perversion of nationalism in Israel. Kahane's "Jewish idea" spawned the new *biryonim* (zealots). In their view, destruction of Arab property was no great affair. Smashing windows and solar heaters and bottles, puncturing car tires – these became everyday behavior. And who are they to talk about threats, curses, and denunciations of political opponents? ["Terrorism with a Skullcap," *"Ve-eleh Shenot..."* (Tel Aviv, 5757), 309]

Kibbutz Movement

There is a large public in Israel today which is psychologically ready to hear God's word, and they expect to hear some sort of message from religious Jewry. For our many sins, owing to our exaggerated emphases, with everyone concentrating on only one area, we are disappointing them. ["A Political Message or an Educational Message," *Alon Shevut* 100 (5743), 49]

∾◦∾

I am extremely disturbed by what is happening in the kibbutz movement. It is a camp that contributed greatly towards the building of *Eretz Yisrael*, and to this day has been a great source of pioneering manpower. The number of military pilots and combat officers that has emerged from this camp is far greater than the average among the country's other population sectors. The voices that have recently emerged from this camp frighten anyone who views things in the long term. There has been a transition to the contemporary political squabbling, which is destroying everything good in the nation. More than all the expressions of hatred, the anger, and the collapse of the Zionist banner, I am frightened by the increasing expressions of despair. I see before me a public that is exceedingly despairing. ["A Political Message or an Educational Message," *Alon Shevut* 100 (5743), 49]

Major vs. Minor Issues

In all spheres there are differences of degree and level. There are major issues and minor issues. Even when it comes to major issues, there are different levels of importance. In the realm of sanctity, too, there is the *Kodesh* (Holy), and there is the *Kodesh ha-Kodashim* (Holy of Holies). The world of values is likewise structured like a ladder: there are the more important values, and there are less important values. A person's stature and wisdom are measured by his ability to live by a scale of values whose order is established in accordance with the truth of Torah: "a ladder that is placed on the ground and whose top reaches the heavens" (*Bereshit* 28:12). This is the ladder of God; the righteous shall ascend it. ["'On Aharon's Heart' – In Memory of Aharaleh Friedman, *z"l*," *Alon Shevut* 108 (5748), 11]

Minorities

We must remember how the Sages regarded the episode of the Givonim (*Yehoshua* 9). Despite the fact that Yehoshua's oath had no halakhic validity, since it was based on the deception perpetrated by the Givonim, the Israelites did not kill them because of the desecration of God's Name that this would have involved (*Gittin* 46a). The obligation of sanctifying God's Name and refraining from desecrating it require the fulfillment of every promise that is made by the leaders of the nation pertaining to the welfare of non-Jews. I am not aware of any more public, national promise than Israel's Scroll of Independence, which was signed by all the leaders of the State, and which explicitly promises equal rights to all non-Jewish minorities. This official promise, then, has obligatory halakhic weight, based on the mitzva of *kiddush Hashem* and the prohibition of *chillul Hashem*. Our attitude towards the nations of the world is based on five principles: "Beloved is man, who was created in God's image" (*Avot* 3:14); cleaving to the attributes of the Holy One, Blessed be He, Who is beneficent to all; the principle that the Torah's "ways are ways of pleasantness, and all of its paths are peace" (*Mishlei* 3:17); the universal destiny of *Am Yisrael* to be "a light unto the nations" (*Yeshayahu* 49:6), to spread God's word among the nations and to teach them God's ways; and the great principle of creating *kiddush Hashem* and avoiding *chillul Hashem*. ["The Torah's Attitude towards Minorities within the State of Israel," *Daf Kesher* 200 (5750)]

Modesty

There is nothing more beautiful than modesty – not trying to make an impression, not that which is external, but that which is internal. That is the yardstick. A person who feels that for him, the exterior appearance is of prime importance, must work on himself. ["Entering Elul," *Alon Shevut Bogrim* 4 (5755), 42]

∽∘∼

The following story is told of the Rebbe of Mezeritch: A stranger once came and knocked on his front door. The Rebbe asked, "Who is there?" The response was, "I." The Rebbe was shocked that a Jew could utter "I" so easily. The Rebbe opened the door and invited the stranger inside. He asked if he had eaten yet and, upon receiving an answer in the negative, told the guest, "Go to such-and-such a place, a certain distance from here, and eat there." Since the Rebbe had instructed him thus, the Jew went on his way. The road was long and tiring, and he walked and walked, becoming covered with dust along the way. After a hard journey he arrived at the place, filthy and exhausted. A wedding was just about to begin in the village and, as was the custom, a festive meal was offered at the site for the poor. The man joined the poor guests and ate with them. At the end of the meal it was discovered that a silver spoon was missing. Immediately, all suspicion was focused on this Jew, since he was the only stranger, and everyone turned to him accusingly: "You are the thief!" The Jew replied, "Not I!" They

continued to torment him and accuse him, and he stead-
fastly repeated, "Not I! Not I!" Eventually he managed to
escape from them, and started his journey back towards the
Rebbe, wondering all the way what the Rebbe's reason
could have been for sending him to that place. He arrived
at the Rebbe's house, knocked on the door, and once again
the Rebbe asked, "Who is there?" The Jew was about to
answer "I" as he had been accustomed to do, but suddenly
he caught himself and answered, "Not I." Only through
suffering and pain had the message penetrated his consciousness – now he knew that he was "not I." There is only
one "I" – and that is "He." ["And You Shall Know that I am
God," *Daf Kesher* 319 (5752)]

Murder of Prime Minister Yitzchak Rabin

We are obligated to rend our garments over the desecration of God's Name. Have we become like Sedom and Amora? The Jewish people, who taught the world absolute morality, beginning with the prohibition on murder; the Jewish state, the only democracy in the Middle East, a nation founded on the vision of redemption – now resembles some Third World banana republic. This obligates us in *keria* (tearing), if not in rending our clothes, then in rending our hearts. What has happened to us? ["On the Assassination of Prime Minister Rabin, *z"l*," *Alei Etzion* 4 (5756), 14]

～○～

Sadly, the *chillul Hashem* in this case is made worse by the fact that it was perpetrated by someone who regards himself as religious, and he justifies his actions by invoking commandments from the Torah. From a more general perspective, we are guilty in our education of an entire generation towards superficial thinking that is built on slogans and clichés. Our youth are incapable of seeing and understanding a complex reality. In the *yeshivot*, they engage in Talmud study with deep, complex thought; at university they are taught to analyze a text in a complex, serious way; but in political matters, the public atmosphere educates towards shallowness and superficiality. ["Soulsearching," *Alon Shevut Bogrim* 8 (5756), 11]

Natural Morality

God created man "in His image" (*Bereshit* 1:27), endowing him with moral sensitivity and a conscience – in other words, with natural morality. This sensitivity has characterized man ever since the world was created, even when it did not stem from a direct Divine command. God addresses man through his conscience and morals. [*Jewish Values*, 19]

౻∞౼

According to one commonly-held opinion, after the Torah was given, natural morality lost its validity, such that nothing in the world has binding force other than the Torah. This approach assumes that allowing room for natural morality diminishes the importance of Torah, in that it recognizes an additional source of obligation alongside the Torah. According to this point of view, which zealously tries to defend the honor of the Torah, there is no connection between God, Creator of man, and God, Giver of the Torah, as if that which God implanted in man's heart does not belong to God. There are those who prefer that all obligations be derived solely from the Torah and that no significance be attached to any human element. This approach weakens natural morality. Rav Avraham Yitzchak Kook viewed this as a very negative development (*Orot ha-Kodesh* III, *Rosh Davar*, 11): "Fear of Heaven such that, without its effect on the living, people would be more inclined to doing good and realizing that which is beneficial to both the individual and the community, and where, because of its effect this active force diminishes – such fear of Heaven is unfit." Even after the Torah was given, natural morality retains its special role of guiding man in all his paths. [*Jewish Values*, 23-24]

Non-religious Jews

There were times when the hatred of the Jews on the part of the nations of the world was directed in particular toward Jews who observed Torah and *mitzvot,* and not towards Jews who accepted upon themselves the religion of their host nation. In our day, this is no longer true. The Jew is hated for being a Jew, irrespective of his actual beliefs. When the hatred of Jews ignores the opinions and actions of the individual Jew, then the love of the Jewish people must be directed at every Jew qua Jew, without regard for his views and deeds. It is unthinkable that non-Jews should regard a particular person as a Jew, while we relate to him, God forbid, in a negative and alienated manner. In Auschwitz, they did not check people's *tzitzit* before sending them to the gas chambers; should we check *tzitzit* before regarding someone as a brother? [*Jewish Values*, 187-188]

✺

If we have not yet been infected by the *"charedi* heresy," which excludes God from the history of the reestablishment of Jewish statehood and regards it as a purely human act, then we had better realize that the State of Israel is not going to endure if cordial relations do not prevail between all sectors of the nation. Only if Jews relate to each other as brothers, irrespective of ideology, can we maintain this State. Otherwise, we live under a threat of destruction. I have no need for source texts to prove this. Concerning such instances, the Sages have already said, "Why do I need a quotation from Scripture? It stands to reason" (*Bava Kamma* 46b). ["A Torah Perspective on the Status of Secular Jews Today," *Alei Etzion* 2 (5755), 45]

∽◦∾

"God is close to all who call upon Him, to all who call upon Him in truth." So it is written in *Tehillim* (145:18). "To all who call upon Him in truth" – whether they are religious or non-religious. Neither I, as *Rosh Yeshiva*, nor my students and colleagues, your brothers in arms, represent God more than they do. ["Do Not Fear, Israel, for I am with You," *Ha-Ma'alot mi-Ma'amakim*, 39]

∽◦∾

After the assassination of the prime minister, we hear many people quoting Rav Kook *zt"l*, who said that just as the Second Temple was destroyed because of *sinat chinnam*, baseless hatred (*Yoma* 9b), so will the Third Temple be built because of *ahavat chinnam* (baseless love). But why call it *ahavat chinnam*? Are there not many others – yes, even among the non-religious – who deserve our love? There are many dedicated members of our society who certainly fall into that category: members of the security services who vigilantly protect us, boys who give three years to the army, doctors who work for meager wages rather than seek their fortunes overseas, and many others. If someone does not share our religious commitment, it does not mean he has no values, and it does not mean that he has no just claim to our love. ["On the Assassination of Prime Minister Rabin," *Alei Etzion* 4 (5756), 16]

෴

It is a mistake to think that in our generation everything is black. Thirty years ago everything was holy, and now suddenly nothing is holy? Suddenly everything is *treif*, everything is disqualified? Based on the teachings of Rav Kook, in the past people were able to find an element of sanctity even in the ardently secular *Ha-Shomer ha-Tza'ir* movement; is there truly nothing left today? There is room to re-think this and to evaluate the situation differently. ["The Significance of Rav Kook's Teachings for Our Generation," *Alon Shevut Bogrim* 8 (5756), 138]

෴

We must put a halt to the delegitimization of the other side. We cannot deny that amongst *Am Yisrael* there is a worrying phenomenon of absolute secularization and alienation from the values of Judaism and of morality in general. However, it is specifically for this reason that we must take care not to identify this phenomenon and the political views of those who manifest it as one and the same thing. It is very easy to present the opposing view as a "Hellenistic" one, since this exempts us from the need to address that view directly and honestly. It is really true that anyone who regards peace accords as the only solution to the Intifada and to the long and ongoing conflict, with all of its ramifications, is devoid of any values? Is it really true that anyone who is fearful of future bloodshed and believes that this road holds fewer dangers than any other, is indeed a Hellenist? ["Challenges of a New Reality," *Alon Shevut Bogrim* 1 (5754), 76] ɤᴏɤ

I am inclined against maintaining the current status-quo, both because of the problems created by the *aliya* of so many immigrants who are not Jewish – problems which cannot be solved within the current political framework – and because of the constant rise in the number of couples who are looking for alternative weddings. Until now I supported the possibility of civil marriage being extended only to those disqualified from being married according to Halakha, but today I believe that it is possible to make this option available to whoever seeks it. I believe that only a small minority within Israeli society, other than those who are halakhically disqualified, will forgo a wedding "in accordance with the law of Moshe and Yisrael." For this reason, allowing civil marriage will not cause any real damage to the Jewish character of Israeli society. On the contrary, many of those who choose the route of civil marriage today do so as a rebellion against religious coercion and the religious establishment. We may hope that with a lowering of the motivation to rebel, on the one hand, and the increased supply of young rabbis who conduct weddings in a manner that is compatible with young secular couples, on the other, the number of instances will shrink even further. ["Civil Marriage – Yes, Reform – No," *Meimad* 10 (5757), 6]

"Now-ism"

[There is a] wish to solve all problems as quickly as possible – now and immediately, along the lines of "Peace Now" and "*Mashiach* Now." Dealing with social problems by means of education and public awareness is a long and arduous process. The presentation of the problem in the *Knesset* and subsequent appropriate legislation – or at least the transfer of the issue to one of the *Knesset*'s subcommittees – gives the appearance that the problem is being solved quickly and efficiently. ["The Social Challenges Confronting the State of Israel," *Alei Etzion* 10 (5761), 17]

Peace

To the extent that religious Zionist Jewry is conscious of its historical destiny at this difficult time, it must change direction and change tactics. It must declare that we seek peace, and we mean a true and final peace. Not a formal peace with political etiquette, which has recently begun to be regarded as the be-all and end-all, but rather a peace that will remove the fear of the horrors of war. For the sake of such a peace we will be ready to make concessions, including territorial compromise. If such a peace will indeed come about, then there will be moral and halakhic justification for our concessions. Unfortunately, I do not see any chance of such a peace in the visible future, but at the same time we must emphasize this over and over. We must speak about peace as a Jewish value according to the Torah. This is important from an educational and moral perspective, from a Jewish and national perspective, and from a pragmatic perspective within *Am Yisrael* and within the international community. We must hold onto our sharpened sword, but we must keep in its scabbard and not use it other than in times of real need, when there are no other possibilities. ["A Political Message or an Educational Message," *Alon Shevut* 100 (5743), 52]

∾o∾

The Rambam writes (*Hilkhot Chanukka* 4:14), "Great is peace, for the entire Torah was given to make peace in the world, as it is written (*Mishlei* 3:17): 'Its ways are ways of pleasantness, and all of its paths are peace.'" These words, summarizing the Jewish world-view with regard to the value of peace, occupy a central place in my religious consciousness. At the same time, I must admit that this is not what led me to my political views. Far be it from me to be carried away by visionaries who promise us absolute peace. I merely wish to avoid war. A war in our days, even if it would end in Israeli victory, could be catastrophic, God forbid, if we take into account the weapons of mass destruction that are in the hands of the enemy and their range. This, too, we learned from the Yom Kippur War and from the [First] Lebanon War – the national, social and political ramifications of the price of victory. Any political agreement between Israel and the Arabs must involve painful compromise. Talking about political agreements with no territorial compromise has no bearing on reality. At best, it reflects the view that there can be no peace until the coming of the *Mashiach*. Otherwise, it is simply lip-service that is devoid of any substance. ["Challenges of a New Reality," *Alon Shevut Bogrim* 1 (5754), 70]

Peace as a lofty value is not disqualified from being a value because of the use made of it by various groups for political purposes. ["A Political Message or an Educational Message," *Alon Shevut* 100 (5743), 43]

If a chance came about for real peace with the Arabs, and in the wake of this there were chances of halting emigration and nurturing a great movement of *aliya*, and we were faced with the question of which is preferable – more Jews in *Eretz Yisrael* with less of the Holy Land under Jewish rule, or fewer Jews in *Eretz Yisrael* with more of the Holy Land under Jewish rule, I would choose the first option. I perceive the importance of this declaration not on the practical level, nor from the political perspective, but rather in the educational sphere; therefore, I regard it not as a political message, but rather as an educational one. To my mind, the time has come – and I hope that it is not too late – for such a declaration to be made openly. ["A Political Message or an Educational Message," *Alon Shevut* 100 (5743), 43]

Permissiveness

All of the expressions of permissiveness that manifest themselves, even in a civilized manner, have profound ramifications. Anyone with understanding of the psychology of the soul knows that it is impossible to free oneself from it. Every expression of identification – even if the person does not identify in principle with permissiveness, but nevertheless imitates it in an outwardly careless appearance – will ultimately seep into his consciousness. Indeed, one might say: what value is there to external appearance, when a person can go about freely? But when this is accompanied by defiance, a war against society's conventions, then it is idolatry! We must fight against this. All of Judaism is about frameworks; nowhere have I found any defense of permissiveness and its accoutrements. ["Permissiveness and Its Accoutrements," *Alon Shevut Bogrim* 2 (5754), 102]

Politics

Politics is not my profession. I assume that others may see things differently, and they have other suggestions, too. I accept any political view as legitimate if it is based on a view of all of *Eretz Yisrael* as living flesh, as a limb of our body; on the view of the good of *Am Yisrael* as taking precedence over the good of *Eretz Yisrael*; and on the view of peace as a Jewish value of great importance. ["A Political Message or an Educational Message," *Alon Shevut* 100 (5743), 53]

≈≈≈

In every public debate there is a phenomenon of personal feelings becoming involved. It is natural that many of my friends in the "Greater Israel" camp consider themselves offended. Since they are looking at the situation through personal lenses, they perceive the injury on the level of the ideal. I believe that to the extent that I have brought harm to the Greater Israel camp, I have at the same time done a favor to the Greater Israel cause. As a *Rosh Yeshiva*, I would certainly prefer to keep away from any public controversy, but I acted as did out of a sense of "a time to act for God" (*Tehillim* 119:126). Far be it from me to tell my students, "Accept my opinion," but if the only thing that comes of my words is a clarification of ideas and an open debate, without fear of anyone, then that will be my reward. ["A Political Message or an Educational Message," *Alon Shevut* 100 (5743), 53]

Prayer

The emphasis on the emotional element in prayer, prayer with intensity and enthusiasm, finds expression in the growing popularity of "Carlebach *minyanim.*" As opposed to this view, Rav Nachman of Breslov, who sought to raise the level of Divine service among simple Jews, always taught that one should invest effort in being joyful, in song and dance – not as an expression of closeness to God, in the spirit of the classical approach, but rather as a means through which a person might achieve such closeness. These two approaches receive expression in *Midrash Tehillim* (24:3): "Every place where it is written 'A psalm of David' [e.g., 3:1], it refers to his playing music, and thereafter the Divine Spirit would rest upon him. Where it says, 'Of David, a psalm' [e.g., 24:1], the Divine Spirit would rest upon him, and thereafter he would play." Obviously, we are still very far from the music of King David and from the Divine Spirit that would rest upon him. Nevertheless, under certain conditions, the *midrash* may serve as a source of inspiration. If and when singing and dancing lead a person to open his heart in prayer, to a deepened sense of standing before God Who hears every word directed to Him, to an ability to pour out one's innermost heart, and as a result his heart contains greater joy, in keeping with the verse, "Let my words be sweet to Him; I shall rejoice in God" (*Tehillim* 104:34) – if all these emotions are the result of song and dance, then the teaching of our Sages concerning the "psalm of David" may indeed serve as a source of inspiration for those who follow the path of Rav Nachman in this regard. ["Insight and Emotion in Torah and Prayer," *Alon Shevut Bogrim* 14 (5761), 13]

∞

In prayer, we must not belittle one's honest aspiration to reach the desired level of devotion, even if it does not achieve the desired results. Just as the Holy One, Blessed be He, does not withhold the reward for appropriate speech (*Nazir* 23b), so we believe that He does not withhold reward for an appropriate aspiration. Without this positive aspiration, at the very least, it would be difficult to come to terms with the prayer formula adopted in new *minyanim*, which include some innovations in contrast with the traditional – or even the Chasidic – prayer services. At the same time, we must be cautious when it comes to those feelings of closeness and emotion that are inspired by Eastern religions, which pride themselves on the power of their religious experience. The Eastern mystics are apathetic towards social, human problems and they have no interest in perfecting the world, no aspiration for justice and righteousness. Religious experiences are their entire world; they are the goal in and of themselves; they lead to nothing else. ["Insight and Emotion in Torah and in Prayer," *Alon Shevut Bogrim* 14 (5761), 14]

∞

Concerning the verse in *Yechezkel* (37:4), "Dry bones, hear the word of God," the Gemara (*Sanhedrin* 92b) comments as follows: "Rabbi Yirmiya bar Abba taught: These symbolize people who lack the vitality of God's command." In the wake of the sense of dryness there comes a thirst for something spiritual, for something that moves and stirs. Hence the popularity of *minyanim* where singing and dancing become a central element in prayer, with the expectation that this will lead to a certain sense of upliftment. Rav Nachman sought to turn his teachings into prayers. Indeed, his disciple, Rav Natan, fulfilled his request with ten teachings that he adapted into prayers. It would appear that the time has come to think about how to turn prayers into teachings. ["Insight and Emotion in Torah and Prayer," *Alon Shevut Bogrim* 14 (5761), 17]

∾∘∾

The greatness of a Jew's personality is measured by the depth of his connection to prayer. The prayer is the person! As Rav explains (*Bava Kamma* 3b), "'*Maveh*' means man," based on the verse (*Yeshayahu* 21:12): "If you will inquire (*tivayun*), inquire." The inquirer, the seeker of God, the one who prays – this is the nature of humanity. ["'On Aharon's Heart' – In Memory of Aharaleh Friedman, *z"l*," *Alon Shevut* 108 (5748), 3]

∾∘∾

Man, who was created in the image of God, enjoys an enormous privilege in that God has made it possible for him to pray. Humanity would look different – more sad, more dejected – were it not for this privilege which has been bestowed upon us... Let me share with you a conversation I had with the director of a large retirement home in Miami. The residents' children all lived far away – New York, Washington, Chicago. There were three categories of children. Some sent a check every month to their parents. Sometimes the son or daughter would include a short note, sometimes not even that. In any event, the parent knew that the child remembered him or her every month. Others sent the monthly check straight to the retirement home office; it didn't go to the parent, but at least they remembered their parents every month. The third type, explained the director, were those who made use of a standing bank order, such that the money was sent each month by a teller at the bank without the child having any idea as to whether his parent was even still alive. Everything was conducted automatically. This was the difference between Ya'akov and Esav. God told Ya'akov, "You have to ask every time. You'll receive nothing without asking." Esav, on the other hand, enjoyed the benefits of a "standing bank order." [*Jewish Values*, 117, 121]

∽o∾

The psalmist (109:4) says, *"Ani tefilla"* – literally, "I am prayer." *Tefilla* is expressed in the personality of the individual. If you wish to know something of a person's character – watch him at prayer. [*Jewish Values*, 121]

∽o∾

The first thing that prayer requires is openness – openness towards oneself. Sometimes people think, "So-and-so isn't open towards others." But many people are closed even towards themselves. Everyone – parents, teachers, rabbis – asks his children or students, "How are you doing?" and the standard response is, "Fine." You can't talk to them or engage them. They are closed not only towards others, but also towards themselves. They cannot look inwards. In order to "open up" in front of God, a person first has to "open up" to himself. He should not be satisfied with merely reciting the prayers that appear in the *siddur*; he should add petitions of his own – even if only in his heart. We start our recitation of the *Amida* with the words, "O God, open my lips, and my mouth will declare Your praise" (*Tehillim* 51:17). According to many authorities (see *Be'ur Halakha*, 111, s.v. *Chozer ve-omer*), this is an integral part of *tefilla* itself. "Open my lips" – in other words, open my heart. I feel "closed;" my heart refuses to disclose itself. [*Jewish Values*, 122]

✧

There are those who invest an enormous amount of energy in bodily movements during prayer, convinced that they will thereby drive away foreign thoughts. True, one is permitted to sway slightly during prayer (*Mishna Berura* 48:5), but some people think that in order to arouse profound *kavvana* (concentrated devotion), one has to sway mightily. Yet, clearly, physical movement alone lacks the power to solve a spiritual problem. When King David said, "I shall pour out my complaint before Him" (*Tehillim* 142:3), he was not referring to jumping and moaning, but rather to flowing and natural prayer. [*Jewish Values*, 125]

Questioning

We believe that our holy Torah conveys messages that are relevant to every generation. One may ask – how can this be? The Torah is eternal and unchanging, while generations are constantly undergoing change! The *Chiddushei Ha-Rim* offers the following answer: "'Understand the years of every generation' (*Devarim* 32:7) – in every generation, and in every era, there comes a new understanding of the Torah from heaven, suited to the generation, and the righteous scholars of every generation understand the Torah as is necessary to teach the people of the generation." Every generation has its teachers, its righteous people, its rabbis. In order for them to exert themselves and search until they find the new understanding that is required for the generation, they need to address the problems of the generation, the questions that are asked honestly. Only questions can give rise to answers. If a generation does not know how to ask, its righteous leaders will not know how to answer. ["Insight and Emotion in Torah and in Prayer," *Alon Shevut Bogrim* 14 (5761), 16]

∽o∾

Our generation is one that "does not know how to ask," to use the terminology of the Passover *Haggada.* Not only does it not know how to ask; thanks to the prevailing educational ideology, it doesn't even know what asking is. The phenomenon of "not knowing how to ask" has become an educational ideal for some. Whether consciously or unconsciously, those responsible for educating the younger generation of religious Zionist students viewed the nurturing of this ideal of "not knowing how to ask" as guaranteeing the continuation of their own religious and Zionist approach. The youth – who, by nature, know how to ask – learned to suffice with questions in rather limited areas, areas in which the questions are not significant ones, but rather technical and formal – certainly not existential questions. Beyond these areas, the youth internalized the educational message that questions, if not actually forbidden, are certainly not desirable. Thus there came about a process by which a considerable portion of the youth ceased to ask – not because they were afraid to ask, but simply because they did not know how to. ["Insight and Emotion in Torah and in Prayer," *Alon Shevut Bogrim* 14 (5761), 15]

∽o∾

Today, the religious Zionist public is open, for the better and for the worse, to everything that is going on in the world – in terms of culture, society, science, and communications. In this situation, it is most doubtful whether an educational ideal of "not knowing how to ask" can maintain itself in the long run. ["Insight and Emotion in Torah and in Prayer," *Alon Shevut Bogrim* 14 (5761), 16]

∽o∾

Unquestionably, since the end of the era of prophecy, there are many questions for which we have no answers. There are also questions whose answers are complex and difficult for those who are used to hearing easily digestible slogans. But we have to know that the very possibility of asking,

and the courage to ask – even when the question remains
unanswered – is valuable. "The question of a wise person is
half of the answer" (Rav Yosef Karo, as cited in *Shut Mabit*
I:110). The questions – even the most difficult ones – make
our worship of God more existentially meaningful; they
manifest concern for Torah and *mitzvot*, thus lending to our
divine service depth. Suppressing the possibility of asking,
in contrast, leads to a general shallowness in our service of
God. ["Insight and Emotion in Torah and in Prayer," *Alon
Shevut Bogrim* 14 (5761), 16]

Rabbis

It is inappropriate for rabbis to voice their opinions in areas that fall outside of their expertise, e.g., in medical or financial matters. There are times when expressing opinions in these areas can cause great damage. Many mundane matters are far removed from a rabbi's education and training. It goes without saying that this in no way detracts from his standing. The role of a rabbi – "Provide yourself with a *rav*" (*Avot* 1:10) – centers around matters of Halakha and issues pertaining to Torah, the fear of Heaven and service of God. He is also expected to offer general guidance and counsel. But a rabbi must educate his students in such a way that they develop the capacity to decide significant issues on their own. [*Jewish Values*, 220]

Rav Kook

When I made *aliya*, at the end of World War II, I was looking for a yeshiva where I could study. I went into Merkaz
Ha-Rav for just a few days, and then to Yeshivat Chevron,
where I spent almost two weeks, without introducing
myself, just to get a taste of the place. Having been
impressed by the atmosphere, I decided to remain there,
and I went to present myself to the *Mashgiach* (spiritual
director), *z"l*. He asked me: "What kept you going during
the Holocaust, such that you remained a *yeshiva bochur*?" To
prevent any misunderstanding as to where I belonged, I
told him: "I had a booklet by Rav Kook; that's what sus-
tained me." ["The Significance of the Teachings of Rav
Kook for Our Generation," *Alon Shevut Bogrim* 8 (5756),
136]

∽∘∾

One of the things that interferes with our understanding of
Rav Kook is that people are afraid to state openly that there
were things Rav Kook did not foresee. This in no way
detracts from his greatness. We have to know that his
Ma'amar Ha-Dor isn't about our generation. A person who
says that it refers to this generation is talking nonsense. Rav
Kook believed that within fifty years, the *Mashiach* would
come, and anyone who reads his books cannot understand
him in any other way. But we didn't merit that – and still
Rav Kook remains the greatest philosopher since, perhaps,
the Rambam. We have to remove this obstruction and

acknowledge that there were things that he did not foresee, just as he did not foresee the Holocaust. ["The Significance of the Teachings of Rav Kook for Our Generation," *Alon Shevut Bogrim* 8 (5756), 136]

❧

There are some groups with whom we share no common language, who pretend to represent the teachings of Rav Kook, but they are not Rav Kook's teachings at all. In all of Rav Kook's Zionist writings there is no mention of the famous teaching of the Ramban concerning the commandment to settle the land (except for one sole instance, concerning the sabbatical year). If we are speaking of Rav Kook, then we must get to know him as he is, and not as he is disguised these days. If we get to know him as he is, we can discover whole worlds. The most common term in Rav Kook's writings is not *"Eretz Yisrael,"* but rather *"musar"* (morality). Who today speaks about Rav Kook's moral teachings? ["The Significance of the Teachings of Rav Kook for Our Generation," *Alon Shevut Bogrim* 8 (5756), 137]

❧

Here, a point of paramount importance must be emphasized: we dare not avoid testing Rav Kook's position against the reality of historical events that have transpired since his lifetime. He wrote explicitly that "very soon" it would be possible to run a state on the basis of justice and integrity, because the world would reach a level that would no longer necessitate improper governmental behavior. Rav Kook wrote this approximately eighty years ago. Over the course of these eight decades, have we come any closer to the utopian reality he depicts? Rav Kook was convinced that the corrupt Western culture would collapse after the First World War. The end had finally arrived, he presumed, to the culture of falsehood that was based on deception and crookedness. Did Rav Kook imagine – was he capable of imagining – that World War I would not be the most horrible of wars? Rav Kook's optimism is the optimism before Auschwitz and Hiroshima. ["The Religious Significance of the State of Israel," *Alei Etzion* 14 (5766), 13-14]

∽o∾

My spiritual outlook is based on and nourished by the writings of Rav Kook. But specifically because of what I learned from his teachings, I believe that we, the followers of his approach, must view the current situation in accordance with reality, and not quote passages written eighty years ago without considering their applicability to our period. ["The Religious Significance of the State of Israel," *Alei Etzion* 14 (5766), 18-19]

∽o∾

Distorted use has been made of the teachings of Rav Avraham Yitzchak Kook, *zt"l*, who was among the most prominent of authorities of all times to institutionalize the value of loving fellow Jews – from the perspective of religion, philosophy, morality and Divine service. This distortion causes great anguish to those who were nourished from his pure springs. ["The Nation Grows Mighty While Its Discourse Grows Weak," *Ammudim* 563 (5753), 204]

Redemption

We are commanded to live with the faith that, since the beginning of the modern return to Zion, there is no going backwards. There may be temporary "concealments," but no going backwards. All roads – paved or unpaved – lead to the redemption of Israel. ["On the Significance of the Yom Kippur War," *Ha-Ma'alot mi-Ma'amakim*, 11]

∽◦∾

Some people claim that since this is a Divine process of redemption, even though it is a slow process of "little by little" (*Yerushalmi, Yoma* 3:2), nevertheless the results are fixed in advance – not only in relation to the end of the process, but also that success is guaranteed at each and every stage. Based on this perception, they believe that there is no obligation to take into account the actual reality, potential dangers, the political, social and economic situation, or delays that may occur along the way. For them, it is an unconditional divine process that does not depend on whether the nation follows the divine demands set out in the Torah. We must counter this perception with a different one, according to which the only thing that is guaranteed is the end result of the process, while its duration – whether it takes a longer or shorter time – is dependent on our actions and our behavior. Since it is a natural and "this-worldly" process, we have no guarantee that we will meet with success at every stage. The successes and failures depend upon natural factors, acts of commission and omission, the responsibility for which rests with the nation's elected leadership. We believe that Divine Providence guides our path by creating situations and options in all spheres, while the choice of the most preferable option is left – in the absence of prophecy – to the discretion of the political leadership. ["Challenges of a New Reality," *Alon Shevut Bogrim* 1 (5754), 73]

Reform Jewry

We reject outright the path of the Reform movement. What is especially offensive is its perversion of authentic Judaism. From this perspective, Reform Judaism is worse than secularism, and we have some harsh things to say about their move away from the central foundations that are identified with historical Judaism and with Jewish tradition. Moreover, "for three sins of" the Reform movement, "and for four I shall not bring them back" (cf. *Amos* 1:3-2:8): for marrying Jews to non-Jews according to the law of Yisrael, as it were; for performing ceremonies together with Christian ministers; and for instituting marriage ceremonies for same-sex couples. Even if these phenomena do not characterize all Reform rabbis, they have not been banned by the movement. "And for four I shall not bring them back:" for undermining the genealogical system by adopting the principle of patrilineal descent, which determines the Judaism of children according to the father. This is especially grave in view of the chasm that it creates within the Jewish nation – a chasm that is irreparable. ["Civil Marriage – Yes; Reform – No," *Meimad* 10 (5757), 6]

❧

When deciding matters of national import, we must be aware of the fact that for Reform Jews, who represent a considerable portion of American Jewry, the State of Israel and the feeling of belonging to it represent an important focus of Jewish identity. For this reason, their ability to identify with the State is of substantial Jewish value. This value is worthy of serious consideration in planning our actions here. It is vital, as I see it, that the masses of Reform Jews should not feel rejected by the State of Israel and its institutions. Here in Israel, in contrast, the situation is quite different. Identification with the State is self-evident. One might have expected the Reform movement to find ways to contribute towards Israeli society in the realms of Jewish culture and arts; in the fight against simplistic and materialistic atheism, the remains of the Enlightenment and Marxism; and in emphasizing the moral foundations of Judaism. Unfortunately, this did not happen. Thus far, the movement's principal activity has been directed towards the battle against the Orthodox establishment and an attempt to achieve recognition by the authorities of the State. ["Civil Marriage – Yes; Reform – No," *Meimad* 10 (5757), 7]

∽৹৹৶

From a practical perspective, Reform Jews may be permitted democratic expression in most spheres. I refer here to Reform representation, on the basis of the true ratio of their power in synagogues in the various places. This is in contrast to artificial representation by secular parties that attempt to use them for the sake of the battle to separate Judaism from the State. In my view, this will not drastically change their representation, and this approach may be integrated within a much-needed re-organization of the system of religious services in the State as a whole, and in the religious councils in particular. In the sphere of education, too, I believe that they should be permitted to engage in educational activity, with the assumption that this would have a positive Jewish effect on the secular population. On the other hand, I am vehemently opposed to granting legal status to Reform marriage and divorce. ["Civil Marriage – Yes; Reform – No," *Meimad* 10 (5757), 7]

Religious Experience

In the same way that musical and artistic experiences strengthen a person's connection to those realms, so too religious experiences strengthen one's affinity to religion and the service of God. I refer here to any type of religious experience – not only some unique experience associated with a special prayer, a special mitzva or a special time, and not necessarily the experience of communion with God out of religious ecstasy, as emphasized by Chasidic thought, or out of intensive study of ethical texts, as advised by the Musar movement. I am talking especially about the type of religious experience that is quite widespread today, primarily among young people – the religious experience associated with singing and dancing. Such an experience provides a person with emotional satisfaction and spiritual delight, and these feelings drive people to seek out such experiences.

It is precisely for this reason that some authorities have expressed reservations about seeking out religious experiences; they view the search as a quest for personal gratification, rather than true service of God undertaken for the sake of Heaven. In certain circles, any spiritual pleasure accompanying the performance of a mitzva is regarded as a defect in one's service of God. I see no reason to disqualify the religious experience and spiritual satisfaction that may accompany their observance. Admittedly, "*mitzvot* were not given for the sake of pleasure" (*Rosh Ha-shana* 28a) – in the material sense. But as for the spiritual satisfaction that a person enjoys when he performs a mitzva – not only is it not a defect in his performance of the mitzva, but it is even a mitzva in its own right, for which the person will receive separate reward. [*Jewish Values*, 73-75]

⌐∞⌐

Despite the importance of religious experience, a person must not allow himself to be blinded by the elation felt during that experience, to the point that he mistakes it for fear of Heaven. The speed and ease with which a person achieves a religious experience and a spiritual high through song and dance makes it impossible to identify that experience with true fear of Heaven, about which it has been said: "If you seek it like silver, and search for it as for hidden treasures, then shall you understand the fear of God and find the knowledge of God" (*Mishlei* 2:4–5). [*Jewish Values*, 76]

⌐∞⌐

A number of points must be emphasized. First of all, despite all the importance of religious experience, it is meaningful only when it comes from time to time. When such experiences become one's standard fare, they lose their significance and impact. The experience is liable to turn religious feeling into religious excitement. Religious excitement requires an occasional high dosage, because it is not based upon full spiritual content, whereas true spiritual feeling must be connected to the spiritual level of the person. Second, the impact of a religious experience is passing and short-lived. The most profound religious experience that the Jewish people ever had was the Splitting of the Sea, when they expressed their faith in God through the Song of the Sea (*Shemot* 15). Immediately thereafter, however, we once again hear their complaints (ibid. 16:3): "Would we have died by the hand of God in the land of Egypt, when we sat by the fleshpots and when we ate our fill of bread! For you have brought us out into this wilderness to kill this whole congregation with hunger!" Further on, they again complain (ibid. 17:3): "Why is it that you have brought us out of Egypt, to kill us and our children and our cattle with thirst?" The religious experience associated with the Splitting of the Sea quickly passed, and the people of Israel returned to their sinful behavior and harsh words towards Moshe, Aharon, and God. [*Jewish Values*, 77-78]

∽∘∾

Another problem connected to the experiential realm stems from the fact that we are dealing with an external phenomenon, and as such, it is liable to be artificial. People sometimes behave in a manner that appears to flow from an internal experience, but in truth, their conduct is purely external, motivated by a desire to be part of a certain atmosphere or to be seen as a spiritual person. As in any other realm that is primarily externalization, great care must be taken not to lose the required sincerity. [*Jewish Values*, 78]

∽∘∾

We have seen that religious experience cannot stand on its own. It is important and significant when accompanied by the primary foundations of Divine worship; it can then deepen that service and strengthen one's identification with it. [*Jewish Values*, 78]

Religious Insecurity

There are approximately thirty thousand Internet responsa given by rabbis affiliated with the Religious Zionist camp. While this phenomenon does express a general thirst for Torah, it at the same time reveals a profound problem. I understand that it is technically easy to "ask" on the Internet, and questions can even be submitted anonymously. Yes, there are simple questions and unnecessary ones; there are ingenious questions and *"klutz kashes."* However, all these questions share a common denominator: they strive to know the position of the Torah regarding this or that phenomenon. Everything revolves around the lifestyle of the Torah observant Jew.

It appears to me that a suppressed and previously hidden problem is surfacing now. While this general thirst for Torah is a positive phenomenon, the fact that it expresses itself through a search for absolute answers from authoritative sources can be viewed as problematic. These questions demonstrate that the Torah observant community has lost its self-confidence in its way of life, its faith, and its values. Therefore it turns to rabbis for a sense of security. This phenomenon is particularly dangerous when it involves parents who have lost their own confidence and worry about their children's Torah observance. Their doubt becomes a self-fulfilling prophecy.

In recent decades, Religious Zionism has done great deeds. We have built the land, expanded its settlement, etc. However, all this great work was accompanied by a sense of confidence and faith in our path. The confidence of the Religious Zionist camp was so great that there were some who heard the drumbeat of redemption. We were awed by our country's military and economical prowess. We came dangerously close to the worship of our own mastery.

Now that the difficulties have begun to surface, doubt has begun to filter into the world of Religious Zionism. In response, the youth rush to follow those who "have answers for every question." One of the graduates of our yeshiva came to me with his son, who proudly informed me that in his yeshiva there is an answer for every question. In our yeshiva, I inform the students upon their arrival that we do not have an answer for every question. One needs the religious self-confidence to live with questions; the prophets too lived with questions. ["Religious Insecurity and its Cures," *Alei Etzion* 15 (5767), 9-10]

Religious Zionism

Religious Zionism was once the bridge between all sectors of the public. Are we now consigned to being, God forbid, a divisive wall? ["The Nation Grows Mighty While Its Discourse Grows Weak," *Ammudim* 563 (5753), 204]

❦

Classic religious Zionism has not collapsed. What has collapsed is the superficial, perverted view that dominated religious Zionism over the past twenty years. There is hope for religious Zionism. There is also hope for Zionist settlement in the liberated territories. In no other period has religious Zionism been so vital to the State as it is today, with the State's Jewish identity in danger. The State of Israel cannot under any circumstances forgo religious Zionism, which is orientated towards the nation with love for fellow Jews and ways that are pleasant. Perhaps, in order for religious Zionism to continue to exist, we must declare the existence of a different religious Zionism, in which there is a more precise hierarchy of values, and in which there is more responsibility and circumspection. We must project a world view that combines hope and security with responsibility and faith. ["Challenges of a New Reality," *Alon Shevut Bogrim* 1 (5754), 74]

❦

The voice of religious Zionism must be heard in the state sphere and in the social sphere. Thank God, *Am Yisrael* already has a home. The question that is being asked today is, "What sort of house will you build for Me?" (*Yeshayahu* 66:1) What will be the character of that home? ["Not Everything is Halakha," *Alon Shevut Bogrim* 13 (5759), 95]

Repentance

One thing warrants caution. Unfortunately, for a long time the perception has taken root amongst religious Jewry – at least, a large portion of it – that repentance is a positive commandment that is incumbent *upon others*. I believe that if God has a claim against anyone, then His claim is first and foremost against those faithful, believing Jews who frequent the *beit midrash*. Were He to demand from others, there would be far weightier matters to demand, and it is doubtful that such demands can ever be made. A person to whom the Name of God is unknown – it is doubtful whether anything can be demanded of him. If there is any claim to be made, then it is against us. ["The Significance of the Yom Kippur War," *Ha-Ma'alot mi-Ma'amakim*, 13]

Responsibility

We need to raise the banner of responsibility. Responsibility is required in many different spheres: responsibility for the psychological and spiritual strength of the public, responsibility towards people who need help and responsibility to seek and find ways in which to contribute. In the words of the Sages, being responsible means being a guarantor: "All of Israel are guarantors for one another" (*Shevuot* 39a). This means that *Am Yisrael*, the Nation of Israel, is a living, human entity, in which every limb is concerned for the welfare of every other and is responsible to do its utmost to improve the other's situation. A sense of responsibility towards others means that a person doesn't look about for a cushion to sit on while his companions are suffering. Moshe Rabbeinu sat upon a rock because he felt himself a partner in the suffering of his brethren (*Midrash Sekhel Tov*, *Shemot* 17:12). Likewise, we are required to feel a sense of partnership and to assume the responsibility of doing what we can to improve society as a whole. ["From Commitment to Responsibility," *Alei Etzion* 12 (5764), 11]

∽◦∾

At the age of fourteen, I arrived at yeshiva in Hungary. The yeshiva was established in a Chasidic town, but the *Rosh Yeshiva* (dean) introduced the study method that was practiced in the Lithuanian *yeshivot*. There were many difficulties. For two years, the number of students alternated between five and seven. From the first day there I felt as though the entire yeshiva rested upon me. This really affected me. I felt I had a responsibility. I couldn't leave the yeshiva even for five minutes. I felt that the yeshiva's entire existence was dependent on my presence and my studies there. Indeed, the yeshiva did grow over the years, and the number of students reached fifty. I, however, retained my sense of responsibility. What will become of you if you lack a sense of responsibility, if you don't care about anything? Responsibility means responsibility towards friends, towards family, towards all of *Am Yisrael*. ["Parting Speech," *Daf Kesher* 18 (5746)]

∽૦∾

I once heard about someone who was planning a special design for a synagogue. The seats were organized in such a way that each person would see only the wood carvings at the front, but not the person standing next to him. When he was asked why he had planned it this way, he answered: "Every person, in prayer, should be alone with God." That is a Christian idea. In synagogues and *battei midrash* (study halls), that's not how it is. In a *beit midrash*, a person sees everyone else; he looks at everyone else, not only physically, but also spiritually. A Jew must see his fellow and feel a sense of responsibility towards him, like a guarantor. Every person must feel that "If I'm here, everyone is here" (*Avot De-Rabbi Natan* 12), and "If I am not for myself, who will be for me?" (*Avot* 1:14). He must be concerned with everything that goes on in the yeshiva, not just his immediate surroundings. ["Parting Speech," *Daf Kesher* 18 (5746)]

∽૦∾

In the past, I used to tell my students before they went out for military service, that alongside the *Benei Akiva* religious youth movement, a *"Benei Kehat"* movement must be established. The role assigned to the descendants of Kehat was "bearing on their shoulders" (*Bamidbar* 7:9) the sacred vessels. It is important that in every society and in every family there be those who feel that the burden of society or the family rests upon their shoulders and who, as a result, will initiate and organize activities on behalf of the community. Various obligations fall upon the community – both interpersonal matters and matters between man and God. In order for these obligations to be fulfilled, individuals must step forward and assume the responsibility of seeing that they are executed. It is a bad sign for any association of people if none of its members is willing to assume this role. When an individual finds himself in such company, he is bound by the well-known obligation: "In a place where there are no men, strive to be a man" (*Avot* 2:5). Rashi (ad loc.) explains: "Strive to occupy yourself with the needs of the community, but in a place where there is a man [fulfilling that role], you should occupy yourself in your Torah." A person is not necessarily required to search for ways to serve the community, but if there is nobody else to fill that niche, the obligation falls upon every person to address those needs. [*Jewish Values*, 157-158]

Rosh Yeshiva

Any *Rosh Yeshiva* who is content to teach Torah to others, but does not study himself, is deficient in his scholarship. We are all teachers as well as students, and not only because "from my students [I have learned] the most" (*Ta'anit* 7a). When we convey messages we also internalize them more deeply. So long as I feel that I am able to say something that will be to the benefit of the Torah, to the benefit of *Am Yisrael* or of *Eretz Yisrael*, I will not refrain from speaking out. So long as I believe that I am able to diminish the desecration of God's name, to increase the glory of Heaven, to bring individuals closer, to save Jews from bloodshed or to save something of *Eretz Yisrael* – I have not refrained from speaking out, for I too was taught that one must listen to the sound of a baby's cry. ["Hearing the Baby's Cry," *Alon Shevut Bogrim* 1 (5754), 83]

Service of God

According to the Mishna (*Shekalim* 1:1), "On the first of Adar, they make a proclamation regarding the *shekalim* (the annual donation to the Temple)." The Talmud (*Yerushalmi*, *Shekalim* 1:1) explains this law as follows: "Why is this done on the first of Adar? In order to allow Israel enough time to bring their *shekalim*, and thus the donations of the office [which provide for the congregational sacrifices beginning a month later on the first of Nisan] will be supplied from the new [funds] on time." The Talmud teaches us that we are obligated to pay for the congregational sacrifices from the new donations that are given to the Temple. The year begins on the first of Nisan (*Rosh ha-Shana* 1:1), and in order to ensure that everything is prepared on time, the collection of the half-shekel is begun a month beforehand, on the first of Adar. The congregational sacrifices of the coming year are then purchased with the money raised through the donation of the half-shekel.

In telling us that we may not worship God with the use of the previous year's donations, this law reveals a profound message. Each new year, each new generation, each new era, is marked by its own donations and its own sacrifices. The worship of God from the lofty spiritual height of the Temple is one that contains deep emotional meaning. Any change or deviation, no matter how slight, is considered significant. The individual can only present a sacrifice which has been purchased from the new funds. That which belonged to the previous year is no longer valid. It has come to the end of its usefulness. [*A World Built*, 132]

꘎

The danger inherent in commanding people lurks at all times, but in a generation that does not know how to ask, that lacks depth in its Divine service, the danger is more tangible. Coercion can weaken the inner dynamic of Divine service, transferring its emphasis entirety to the practical, external level. The "duties of the limbs," as *Chovot ha-Levavot* defines it, will overwhelm the "duties of the heart." The commandments can become dry, devoid of spiritual vitality, of a sense of elevation, of enthusiasm. ["Insight and Emotion in Torah and Prayer," *Alon Shevut Bogrim* 14 (5761), 17]

꘎

Divine service must be built on truth, not on falsehood or fawning flattery. [*A World Built*, 147]

꘎

Naturalness is valuable not only in contrast to coerced observance of *mitzvot*, but also in contrast to artificial observance. The importance of serving God naturally is included in our prayer (in the middle blessing for Shabbat and Festival prayers), "Purify our heart to serve You sincerely." Artificiality constitutes a flaw in the sincere worship of God. The meaning of this prayer is that a person's performance of *mitzvot* should correspond to his internal state of loving God, fearing Him, and seeking His closeness. There should be no disproportion between the quantity of his actions and his internal values. The prayer is directed at filling in what is missing, not in the execution of God's service, but in its spiritual backing. [*Jewish Values*, 88]

Settlement

The government, in seeking to implement peace accords, is obligated to find channels of dialogue with the settlers, to make them aware that it is not neglecting them or treating them as second-class citizens. The government must make it clear that its statements concerning responsibility for the security of the settlers have practical meaning. In this way the government will be able to contribute greatly towards raising the spirits of the settlers and leading them from black despair to new hope. If the feelings of despair continue to intensify, it may be dangerous for society and the country as a whole. ["Challenges of a New Reality," *Alon Shevut Bogrim* 1 (5754), 75]

✧

I am not afraid of the delegitimization of the settlement enterprise by the Left. We do not need their legitimization. It is not by their word that we live our lives. ["Hearing the Baby's Cry," *Alon Shevut Bogrim* 1 (5754), 87]

Social Justice

This phenomenon of freedom from commitment also means freedom from social justice. I am aware that many of the statements which we have heard concerning social gaps and social justice since the establishment of the state have been pure lip-service, but I believe nevertheless that even the lip-service which once existed had its own sort of positive dynamic. I don't believe that one can address the problems arising from social gaps purely out of election-campaign concerns, without emphasizing the importance of social justice as a moral and national value. When there is no commitment to the social aspect, the sense of caring about what goes on in society also disappears. I also think that one cannot speak about hedonistic inclinations and the clear trend towards materialism to which we are witness without mentioning the destructive atmosphere of the feeling of freedom from commitment. I suspect that there is also some connection between the feeling of freedom from commitment and the sense of permissiveness which we regularly encounter.

Allow me to add the following: the first message which Judaism came to convey was that of commitment to justice and righteousness. It is said of Avraham, "For I know him, that he will command his children and his household after him, and they shall keep the way of the Lord, to do justice and righteousness" (*Bereshit* 18:19). ["The Social Challenges Confronting the State of Israel," *Alei Etzion* 10 (5761), 12]

Society

We must educate the nation to be willing to make sacrifices. There is a need to fight materialism, the worship of silver and gold, the evil inclination, and base desires. We cannot ignore all of these problems and focus all of our energies on the battle for *Eretz Yisrael* alone. We are still lacking the moral foundation of readiness to sacrifice something for the sake of values. We must begin from the foundations: to fight against materialism, to raise the moral, religious, Torah, and cultural level of the nation. We cannot talk only about *Eretz Yisrael* while ignoring all the rest. ["This is the Day that God Has Made; We Shall Be Happy and Rejoice in It," *Alon Shevut Bogrim* 3 (5754), 97]

∽∘∾

The chasm between the religious – even the religious Zionists – and the non-religious is deepening. Verbal shallowness, cheapness, vulgarity and violence have penetrated almost every respectable corner of national and public life. Such phenomena are to be found among all strata of the public, including the religious public. Lately we have witnessed too many scandals associated with religious society. We dare not make our work easier by placing the blame on some or other circles. Unfortunately, we must admit that indeed, "Something like a plague has appeared on the house" (*Vayikra* 14:35). Today it is fashionable to destroy every icon, to bring down the nation's heroes – from both the distant and the more recent past, to topple any attitude of respect and admiration towards them. The trend is to dissolve any respect for any respectable institution and for any respectable office-bearer in the public, national or religious sphere. This trend is trickling down, unfortunately, through all layers of society – including religious society. The main problem today is molding society in Israel, molding its Jewish and moral character. Our quest is to present our holy Torah as a significant and relevant element in the shaping of society, to show its eternity and its vitality and its significant grappling with the great and troubling problems of society in our times. This is in contrast to the limited perceptions that border at times on primitiveness but garb themselves in religious attire, phenomena that often lead to a desecration of God's Name amongst us and amongst the public at large. ["The Nation Grows Mighty While Its Discourse Grows Weak," *Ammudim* 563 (5753), 204]

Speaking Out

So long as I feel that I am able to say something that will be to the benefit of the Torah, to the benefit of *Am Yisrael* or of *Eretz Yisrael*, I will not refrain from speaking out. So long as I believe that I am able to diminish the desecration of God's name, to increase the glory of Heaven, to bring individuals closer, to save Jews from bloodshed or to save something of *Eretz Yisrael* – I have not refrained from speaking out, for I too was taught that one must listen to the sound of a baby's cry. [*Alon Shevut Bogrim* 3 (5754), 72]

∽◦∽

I must apologize to this audience for the feelings of embarrassment and discomfort that I caused by giving public voice to my opinion [concerning the massacre in the Lebanese refugee camps of Sabra and Shatilla]. I have come to realize that one's words are treated differently when they are conveyed in the media from when they are uttered within the yeshiva. It is not pleasant to encounter disappointed, surprised looks accompanied, in general, by questions like, "What's happened to your *Rosh Yeshiva*?" I, too, have encountered many expressions of disappointment, and sometimes even reproach – oral and written – along with many expressions of support. On the personal level, to borrow the language of King David, I can accept going about with a feeling of "I have been a stranger to my brethren, and foreign to my mother's children" – simply because "zeal for Your House has consumed me" (*Tehillim*

69:9-10). I believe that those things had to be said for the sake of the honor of Heaven, for the sake of the honor of the Torah, and for the sake of the honor of *Eretz Yisrael*. As for those who feel discomfort, those who do not believe as I do that it is worthwhile, in this instance, to be unpopular – I can only say that I understand their feelings, and I am certain that they understand me, too. ["A Political Message or an Educational Message," *Alon Shevut* 100 (5743), 34]

∽◦∾

There was a reason of significant weight in my decision to make a public statement. I refer to the atmosphere that has been created and nurtured by certain circles, according to which if someone does not accept their views, not only are that person's views unacceptable, but he himself is unacceptable. He is marked with a certain label and immediately identified with marginal groups, and anyone with "true" fear of Heaven, who is firm in his faith, is required to keep away from him. Unfortunately, even great Torah scholars who used to be known as religious Zionist leaders have not been spared such labels, and to the extent that they do not toe the ideological and political line, they have been all but excommunicated. It is a fact that many rabbis and Torah scholars are wary of expressing themselves freely for fear of the label that will be attached to them. ["A Political Message or an Educational Message," *Alon Shevut* 100 (5743), 35]

∽◦∾

There is a strange phenomenon here of a society that is incapable of tolerating a dissenting opinion. You cannot imagine how many calls and letters I receive almost every day, from people attempting to change my opinion. Unfortunately, it exists not only in our society. In *charedi* (ultra-Orthodox) society and among left-wingers, too, dissenting opinions are intolerable. What's so terrible? *Gevald*! So what if there's someone who thinks differently? Are we living in a totalitarian society? ["Hearing the Baby's Cry," *Alon Shevut Bogrim* 1 (5754), 84]

State of Israel

We must reexamine the matter of the Jewish character of the State and think about how to nurture this character without religious coercion, and with an internalization of democratic values. ["Not Everything is Halakha," *Alon Shevut Bogrim* 13 (5759), 95]

∽◦∾

Rav Kook was exceedingly optimistic. He felt confident that the Jewish settlement in the Land of Israel would develop into a model society and serve as a shining example for other countries... Rav Kook's optimistic vision predicted that as Jewish autonomy would develop, so would its moral image. And it is specifically this development, as we saw earlier, that affords the Jewish State its exalted stature and guarantees the correction of past misdeeds. Let us now take an honest look at our society today. Does contemporary Israeli society live up to Rav Kook's vision? Can we say about the State of Israel that "theft, robbery, murder and the like are not even heard of"? The violence, corruption and growing tensions among the various segments of society prove beyond a shadow of a doubt that we have not reached the ideal state of which Rav Kook dreamt long before the establishment of our State of Israel.

When analyzing the significance of our State, must we employ the same terms used by Rav Kook in the context of the ideal state he envisioned? May we do so? Rav Kook's mindset was suffused with a sense of optimism regarding the development of humanity as a whole, on the basis of which he foresaw the moral development of the Jewish collective. Unfortunately – or rather, tragically – this development never occurred. We have to assess the Jewish State as it is, not as Rav Kook wanted it to be, and only then determine where it belongs within our world view. ["The Religious Significance of the State of Israel," *Alei Etzion* 14 (5766), 14-16]

∽०∾

In the past, very grave opinions were expounded regarding the Holocaust. Some people claimed that the Holocaust was a sort of price that the Jewish People had to pay in order that the Jewish State could be established. There are those who claimed that the State of Israel is the Divine compensation for the destruction of the Holocaust. There were even those who claimed that the *Shoah* was the only way – or, at least in practical terms, became the impetus – to compel the Jews of Europe to immigrate to the Land of Israel. These are very difficult claims, approaches that I find hard to countenance at all. [*A World Built*, 145]

∽०∾

Despite the many problems the State faces, we may not ignore the great miracles we experienced at the time of its establishment. Analogously, although the Hasmonean state was far from perfect, its establishment (and the return of Jewish sovereignty, albeit limited) was nevertheless a cause for celebration, as the Rambam emphasizes. The Rambam (Commentary to the Mishna, *Yoma* 1:3) knew very well the inauspicious character of the Hasmonean kings.

Nevertheless, he felt that the establishment of the Hasmonean monarchy constitutes the main reason behind the celebration of Chanukka (*Hilkhot Chanukka* 3:1-3). The Second Temple period thus serves as a legitimate model by which we may assess the contemporary Jewish State, a half-century after its establishment. However imperfect, one cannot overlook the many positive elements of our independent national existence. Our leaders today are no worse than the Hasmonean kings, and our country is no worse than theirs was. On the contrary, our leadership and society often exhibit moral qualities far superior to those of the Hasmonean dynasty. ["The Religious Significance of the State of Israel," *Alei Etzion* 14 (5766), 16-17]

∽∘∾

How can we not thank the Almighty for all the kindness that He has showered upon us? First and foremost, the State of Israel serves as a safe haven for five million Jews. After the nightmare of the Holocaust, hundreds of thousands of Jewish refugees wandered around the globe, finding a home and refuge only in Israel. The State has contributed an incalculable amount to the restoration of Jewish pride after the devastating *chillul Hashem* (desecration of God's Name) caused by the Holocaust. Today, too, the State plays an enormous role in the Jewish identity of our brethren throughout the world. For so many of them, the emotional attachment to the State remains the final thread connecting them to the Jewish people and to the God of Israel. ["The Religious Significance of the State of Israel," *Alei Etzion* 14 (5766), 17]

∽∘∾

I experienced the horror of the destruction of European Jewry, and I can thus appreciate the great miracle of Jewish rebirth in our homeland. Are we not obligated to thank the Almighty for His kindness towards us? Unquestionably! And not just on *Yom ha-Atzma'ut* (Israeli Independence Day); each day we should recite *Hallel* seven times for the wonders and miracles He has performed on our behalf: "I praise you seven times each day!" (*Tehillim* 119:164). ["The Religious Significance of the State of Israel," *Alei Etzion* 14 (5766), 17-18]

✽

Unlike the *charedim*, we will not undermine the importance or legitimacy of the State; but our love for our country must not blind us from criticizing its shortcomings. We remain very, very far from the ideal Jewish State, and we must therefore do whatever we can to bring about its realization. A more just society and stronger communal values are necessary prerequisites for its actualization. If we want to hasten the ultimate redemption, we must work harder to ensure moral values on both the individual and communal levels. Closing the social gaps, concern for the vulnerable elements of society, fighting poverty, respectful treatment of the non-Jews in Israel – all these measures will bring us closer to the day for which we long. ["The Religious Significance of the State of Israel," *Alei Etzion* 14 (5766), 19]

✽

I heard a rumor – and I hope that it's not true – that an important religious Zionist rabbi expressed some doubt as to whether *Yom ha-Atzma'ut* should be celebrated this year.

The moment I heard it, a teaching of our Sages (*Ta'anit* 29a) came to my mind: "'And the people wept on that night' (*Bamidbar* 14:1) – Rabba said in the name of Rabbi Yochanan: That night was the night of Tisha Be-Av; the Holy One, Blessed be He said: 'Your weeping was baseless, so I will set for you weeping for generations.'" A person who sees only "that night," only today, only now, has questions and doubts. But a person with a sense of history knows, like Rabbi Akiva when he saw the fox emerging from the place of the Holy of Holies (*Makkot* 24a-b), that "Old men and women will yet sit in the open places of Jerusalem" (*Zekharya* 8:4). ["This is the Day that God Has Made; We Shall Be Happy and Rejoice in It," *Alon Shevut Bogrim* 3 (5754), 95]

∽o∾

The State of Israel is not a normal country: "Not by their sword did they inherit the land, nor did their arm save them" (*Tehillim* 44:4). Its problems cannot be solved by the sword or by an outstretched arm, because it is a Jewish country. Here the fight is not, as in the case of other nations, over borders. Here we fight for our very existence. For someone who lacks faith, this may lead to despair, but for us this very faith is a source of power and security. ["Not By Their Sword Did They Inherit the Land... But Because You Desired Them," *Alon Shevut Bogrim* 6 (5758), 18]

Stringencies

I was once asked by one of my students why I do not observe a particular stringency, which the *Mishna Berura* recommends that a God-fearing person should practice. I replied: "When you read a section in the *Mishna Berura* that is directed at 'a God-fearing person,' you are convinced that he is referring to you. I have no such presumptions." It should also be noted that the *Mishna Berura* says that it befits one who fears Heaven to practice stringency, but he does not say that such stringency leads a person to fear of Heaven! [*Jewish Values*, 94]

Suffering

None of the troubles and suffering that befall the Jewish nation, in every generation and in every era – including all the troubles and suffering that the Prophets spoke about and that the Sages foresaw with divine inspiration, including the suffering of the "birthpangs of the *Mashiach*" (*Midrash Tanchuma, Parashat Noach* 3), pangs that will be followed by a great birth – none of those troubles and suffering represent a necessary, inevitable reality. Birth can happen without them; as the prophet describes it: "Before she travailed, she gave birth; before her pain came, she was delivered of a son" (*Yeshayahu* 66:7). The fact that redemption can come without suffering, but its arrival is nevertheless accompanied by suffering, obligates us with the positive commandment of crying out, of soul-searching, thinking about our actions, and knowing that the Holy One, Blessed be He, is waiting for our repentance. ["The Significance of the Yom Kippur War," *Ha-Ma'alot mi-Ma'amakim*, 12]

∽∘∾

We have to know that the point of suffering is not only punishment. Suffering cleanses and also educates. Suffering has educational aspects to it, and these aspects may be far removed from those sins that caused the suffering. The educational aspect can initiate the sufferer on a path towards the inculcating of consciousness and sensitivity in a certain area, or in a certain direction – a process which may take a long time, but may also be brief. Obviously, it is entirely up to us. ["The Significance of the Yom Kippur War," *Ha-Ma'alot mi-Ma'amakim,* 17]

Superstition

The attraction of non-rational thought and primitive forms of mysticism is a problem that has taken on national proportions. It seems that a person doesn't need to be religious in order to believe in superstition. Horoscopes have become the rage. Look how many pages they occupy in the Friday newspapers. In certain circles within the religious community, there are a growing number of personalities who supposedly have unlimited wisdom about both heavenly and earthly matters and who are turning the Torah into a modern-day oracle. ["The Social Challenges Confronting the State of Israel," *Alei Etzion* 10 (5761), 15]

 ∽∘∾

I am simply amazed when, every once in a while, people who call themselves rabbis get up and think that they can provide an explanation for every tragedy and every road accident, why it happened and what caused it. Where do these people get the audacity to think that they know something that every other mortal in our generation doesn't know? It makes me very angry. The appearance of this phenomenon amongst the religious community is a sign of shallowness in Torah learning, and amongst society in general it is a sign of cultural shallowness. Where logic ceases to be the criterion, Torah cannot exist; and where the use of logic is made redundant, there cannot be any culture. Only in a place of cultural and spiritual hollowness can a world of fears and imaginary desires take the place of reality and clear judgment. The popularity of mysticism both arises from primitivity and leads back to primitivity. ["The Social Challenges Confronting the State of Israel," *Alei Etzion* 10 (5761), 15]

∽๐๛

Belief in mysticism and magical forces causes people to believe in immediate solutions; every problem must be solved right away, and if it isn't, then someone is to blame, and the guilty party must be condemned. And if a person senses that some problems cannot be solved immediately, that means that he has no solution. The concept of a "process" has fallen into disuse among the general public. Every problem must be solved immediately, and if it cannot be solved by regular means, then pressure must be applied; after all, nothing stands in the way of force. In this way, the use of and reliance on force penetrate and control a wide sector of society. ["The Social Challenges Confronting the State of Israel," *Alei Etzion* 10 (5761), 16]

Tolerance and Pluralism

In a situation where everything is seen in black and white, there is no room for genuine tolerance. If I think white while someone else thinks black, then at the very most we can hope for polite behavior and an avoidance of voicing our true opinions – because if I think it's completely white, and he thinks it's completely black, then he's either an idiot or simply despicable. If he really believes it's black, then sensible and honest people obviously have no business listening to him. True tolerance exists only when a person sees the full picture in all its complexity and sees the various possibilities, the different opinions which could arise from that same picture, and thus recognizes the legitimacy of someone else's opinion. This type of tolerance is the soul of true democracy. "Both are the words of the Living God" (*Eiruvin* 13b) – in other words, both are legitimate; but Beit Hillel even went so far as to mention first the opinions of Beit Shammai, which were opposed to their own. This is true tolerance. ["The Social Challenges Facing the State of Israel," *Alei Etzion* 10 (5761), 13-14]

∞

We must halt the phenomenon of delegitimization of dissenting views within religious Zionism. There are profound disagreements within our camp concerning the hierarchy of values within the triad of *Am Yisrael*, *Torat Yisrael*, and *Eretz Yisrael*. However, we must educate towards mutual respect among the different opinions and presenting the bigger picture to the public in general, and to the youth in particular. ["Soulsearching," *Alon Shevut Bogrim* 8 (5756), 13]

໖ﾟໍ

Every year, students from the yeshiva go to celebrate Simchat Torah together with new immigrants in the development towns. Once I happened upon a student who had just returned from Kiryat Shemona. I asked him: "You went into the synagogue – how did they welcome you?" He told me, "They threw us out, and one old man even reproached us: 'Why are you capering about like goats?'" One has to understand that they have their own way of expressing joy. Every generation has its own way of relating to things. A German Jew once told me that in Frankfurt there were rehearsals for the *hakkafot* on Simchat Torah, because there everything is ceremonial, and the person who will be carrying the Torah scroll has to present himself in a frock coat and top hat. I was young, then, and I laughed: "What do you mean? As if they know what joy is!" Until once I heard my neighbor, who was a German Jew, reminiscing with a friend about the *hakkafot* in Frankfurt. He was moved to tears at the recollection. Thus I discovered that everyone has his own way of expressing feelings. We, too, must look at our generation within its own context. We cannot dismiss any dissenting opinion or any person who does not think the same way as everyone else. ["The Significance of the Teachings of Rav Kook for Our Generation," *Alon Shevut Bogrim* 8 (5756), 138]

Torah Scholars

Showing respect towards a Torah scholar is not dependent on his belonging to some or other camp. It is an independent obligation that is not measured in terms of that scholar's leadership or position at the head of some or other party. It is a path that we must cleave to and which we must inculcate. There must be courtesy towards every Torah scholar. That is respect for Torah. ["What is the Biblical Source for the Concept of *Da'at Torah?*", *Alon Shevut Bogrim* 12 (5758), 101]

Torah Study

If one does not bring Torah into a certain place, other things will enter. Nothing is neutral. There is no room for the statement, "I'm not a *lamdan* (studious one)." If you aren't a *lamdan*, if you don't engage in Torah study, you'll end up engaging in worthless matters. ["Entering Elul," *Alon Shevut Bogrim* 4 (5755), 39]

∽o∾

We do not aspire to disconnect ourselves from communal matters and needs. We are aware of and involved in what is going on in the nation. The whole idea of *"Hesder"* is an expression of this involvement. Indeed, I believe that one cannot be involved in secular society without a strong Torah foundation. Without Torah, we will be left with nothing. The foundation of the Torah is the Oral Law. "The Holy One, Blessed be He, forged a covenant with *Am Yisrael* only for the sake of the Oral Law" (*Gittin* 60b). The foundation of everything is the give-and-take of the Talmudic sages. After them, there is room for studying Bible and Jewish philosophy, but the foundation is the Oral Law. It holds a special, magical secret. Anyone who tries a different route – basing his study mainly on philosophy, Tanakh, or other subjects – is doomed to failure. ["Entering Elul," *Alon Shevut Bogrim* 4 (5755), 40]

∽o∾

One of the strategies of the evil inclination is to instill the feeling that "the *beit midrash* is the answer to everything." You don't need to make any effort; the *beit midrash* will create the atmosphere and influence you. Yet there is no such thing as a month of Elul without the command, "Carve *for yourself*" (*Shemot* 34:1) – you have to do the hard work yourself. Certainly, the atmosphere helps. But someone who builds his life on atmosphere alone ends up living in the air – *luftgescheft* – and has achieved nothing. A person must apply himself. He cannot simply follow his mood. He must rise up to serve God, whether he feels like it or not. He must get to the *beit midrash* on time and open his Gemara, no matter what mood he's in. ["Entering Elul," *Alon Shevut Bogrim* 4 (5755), 41]

❧

Our current generation is one of flux and change. I believe that the "changeability" of our day stems from insecurity. Yet whoever believes that he can heal the ills of our generation through the songs of Reb Shlomo Carlebach, through merely intensifying the emotions, is mistaken. This is like taking aspirin. Its effect is temporary; the enthusiasm it generates is momentary. People will always seek a new thrill. This is not a value that will create the religious stability, security and confidence that is sorely needed. Torah study, on the other hand, is an everlasting value that remains with us long after we close the book. To heal our generation we need stability. We must present two important messages. First, the Torah has not lost an iota of its charm; it is as relevant as ever. The problem lies not in the Torah but in what we have added to it. Second, pain relievers are not enough. We must return to the path of arduous study; we must toil and invest in the acquisition of knowledge. Only if we remember these two values and work towards their achievement, will we be able to ascend the path which leads to the House of God. ["Religious Insecurity and Its Cures," *Alei Etzion* 15 (5767), 12-13]

∞◦∞

It is important for a person to continue with in-depth Torah study his entire life, even after he has left full-time study in the *beit midrash*. This is not only because this is the highest level of Torah study, but because it is in this way that the service of God finds expression in its fullest intensity. In a world where so much importance is attached to the intellect, a person cannot possibly fulfill his obligation by learning *Daf Yomi* or the like, which does not require great intellectual effort. The brain, the seat of the intellect, is man's most important organ. Should we content ourselves with serving God with our hands and other limbs – taking the *shofar* in our hands and blowing it with our mouths, donning *tefillin* and eating *matza* on Pesach – and let our brains lie idle, uninvolved in His service? A person who does not occupy himself in Torah study lacks something very basic in his service of God. Should we leave our brains and intellect for our careers, for acquiring academic degrees, and serve God only with our other limbs? [*Jewish Values*, 49-50]

∞◦∞

A professional craftsman can express his service of God by building a synagogue in a way that makes full use of his talents. However, in a generation that attaches so much importance to the intellect, it is important that the intellect, too, be employed in the service of God. In a period when people invest such great efforts in various fields of study, should the service of God not demand strenuous application of the intellect? Precisely at such a time, it is especially important that Torah study should be serious and in no way inferior in intellectual profundity to other realms of study. The service of God will not survive in our day if its bearers are devoid of Torah scholarship. It is impossible to live a serious religious life without deep Torah learning. [*Jewish Values*, 50]

❧

A person who studies Torah "takes" God with him and creates a bond with Him. Even if we are unable to explain exactly how this bond is created, history proves that without intensive Torah study, nothing will remain. Jewish communities in which there was no Torah study, no occupation with the intricate discussions of Abbaye and Rava, did not survive. Go and look at all the curricular experiments that have been conducted to this day, go and visit all the various *battei midrash*, and you will see that the only institutions to survive are those where Gemara was and continues to be studied. Gemara *shiurim* continue for twenty or thirty years, whereas other classes generally last for a year or two, and then are discontinued. [*Jewish Values*, 53]

❧

From time to time, we should stop and consider the greatness of Torah, its grand teachings, the mighty revolution that it brought to the world. Then we will understand how the small details regarding "an ox that gored a cow" (*Bava*

Kamma 46a) or "the mouth that forbade is the mouth that allows" (*Ketubot* 22a) are part of a gigantic system. A scientist who works on tiny details, on a single atom, on a gene that he succeeds in isolating, understands from them the wisdom that lies hidden in the entire universe. He knows little about what is going on in other areas, but from his recognition of the wisdom inherent in the detail before him, he learns to recognize and understand that this isolated detail is part of a much larger world. The same applies to Torah study. The understanding of the small detail does not exhaust itself in the detail and its content. This detail is part of a way of life, part of a Torah containing morality and wisdom, refinement and uprightness. [*Jewish Values*, 53]

Values

In today's mobile world, people are constantly undergoing change and transition – moving from place to place, from city to city, from country to country, from one place of work to another, and so on. People usually undergo such changes because they wish to improve their social and economic status. Frequently, however, such transitions extract a great spiritual toll. For example, a person may have the opportunity to accept a new position that will lead to material advancement, but will prevent him from regularly participating in Torah classes or congregational prayer, and may even seriously diminish the time that he can devote to his children. Sometimes the job being offered may itself raise an ethical problem; for example, a position in the field of marketing, which may require a certain measure of deviation from the truth, or a situation where accepting the job will harm another person. Such a situation tests a person's commitment to the values he professes. Hence the importance of establishing moral priorities and clinging to them, even when doing so will extract a social and economic price. [*Jewish Values*, 210]

War

There is nothing that should cause us more worry than the possibility of another war – a war that will bring, God forbid, additional casualties and a great community of bereaved families. Every individual casualty wounds the souls of a wide radius of the Israeli population. Beyond this, though, every war weakens the Zionist commitment of masses of Jews in *Eretz Yisrael*. I refer particularly to those Jews who lack faith in the Divine Providence guiding the progress of the return to Zion in our times. These Jews believe in the conventional Zionist ideology that says that Zionism comes to solve the problem of Jewish existence. Every war arouses doubts in them as to the rightness of the cause, and causes them to run off to the stock exchange as an escape from the problems that disturb Jewish life in Israel. Every war strengthens the big question which they cannot answer: "Will the sword consume forever?" (II *Shemuel* 2:26). ["A Political Message or an Educational Message," *Alon Shevut* 100 (5743), 52]

∽∾∽

I am not a prophet. I have made mistakes, just as many people make mistakes. Long ago, I participated in demonstrations against concessions when [American Secretary of State] Kissinger was in Israel, and afterwards I regretted it. After the Six-Day War, Kissinger wanted us to make concessions to Egypt and to withdraw to Bir Gafgafa. Had we listened to him, perhaps the Yom Kippur War would not have broken out, and there would not have been a withdrawal from Yammit and from the Sinai. I'm not saying that I haven't made mistakes. But a Jew who lived through the Holocaust, a Jew who has lived through five wars, is permitted to be fearful of another war. I fear that Hamas will take control of the streets, and Hamas means a connection with Hizbullah and a connection with Iran. Indeed, I have fears – is that so terrible? ["Hearing the Baby's Cry," *Alon Shevut Bogrim* 1 (5754), 84]

Who is a Jew?

Concerning the question, "Who is a Jew," there is a clear answer that is set out in Halakha, which also reflects Jewish tradition throughout the generations. However, it is not this question that is currently under discussion, but rather an amendment to the Law of Return. The number of non-Orthodox converts who move to Israel is limited to a few individuals, yet the emotional baggage associated with an amendment to the Law of Return, in both directions, has brought about a public controversy that exceeds any sense of proportion. A situation has been created – and it grows increasingly acute – whereby hundreds of thousands of people regard themselves as Jewish, in terms of family, society, and nationality, while according to Halakha they are not defined as such. This difficult and genuine problem of a division within the Jewish nation cannot be solved by means of legislation by the Knesset. Supporters of the amendment argue that it will lead to a decline in the number of mixed marriages in the Diaspora. This claim manifests no small degree of hypocrisy: will a young Jewish man in Chicago refrain from marrying a non-Jewish woman because of a law passed in Israel's Knesset? Will an amendment to the Law of Return in Israel's parliament, resulting from party- and coalition-centered considerations, halt the wave of conversions overseas that are performed contrary to Halakha? ["A Problematic and Harmful Amendment," *Yediot Aharonot*, 2.12.1988]

⌣o⌣

The truly important question is what price we will be required to pay for the amendment to the law. Reality indicates that the amendment will cause heavy damage both to the State of Israel and to the Jewish nation. Many Jews in the Diaspora do not observe Shabbat, keep kosher or attend synagogue. For them, their connection to Israel represents a central – if not the sole – element of their Jewish identity. For them, a step back from the State of Israel is a step back from their very existence as Jews. We may say that, from a broad perspective, an amendment to the law will achieve a result that is the opposite of its aim, and in the long term it is even likely to intensify the processes of assimilation. An amendment to the law of "Who is a Jew" has nothing more than declarative value. It seems that its supporters believe that a declarative law, which is not acceptable to most of the public and which is achieved through coalition pressure, will be able to solve the Jewish People's spiritual and existential problems. The appropriateness of this approach should be examined in the broader context of religious legislation. The question that should be asked is whether the Torah will profit from this battle. The answer, to my mind, is an unequivocal "no." ["A Problematic and Harmful Amendment," *Yediot Aharonot*, 2.12.1988]

⌣o⌣

So long as a person, through his lifestyle, fulfills and realizes Jewish values of justice, morality, and compassion, he is bringing part of the Jewish essence to fruition. He is an authentic Jew. Beyond this, there are superficial theists and there are superficial atheists. There is heresy that is faith, and there is faith that is heresy. Heresy that is faith refuses to accept simplistic, superficial belief. One aspect of it could be faith in an overall supreme entity, faith in absolute intelligent design, faith in transcendental experience. Another aspect of it is that historical phenomenon of secular Zionism which drew its core values from Jewish sources: the values of morality, society, justice and equality. ["*Am Yisrael* before *Eretz Yisrael*," *Sevivot* 22 (5749)]

Yeshiva

In years past, there were *yeshivot* that tended to sever their students from their homes. In my opinion, a steep price was paid for this approach. I believe that yeshiva students should remain connected to their families and avoid any type of cut-off. They must be especially careful not to offend their parents against the background of heightened meticulousness in the observance of *mitzvot*. [*Jewish Values*, 215]

∽o∾

Charedi (ultra-Orthodox) ideology maintains that while other disciplines can be acquired even if, while studying them, a person is sometimes engaged in other pursuits as well, Torah can be acquired only by someone who studies it incessantly. They therefore reject the option of *yeshivot Hesder*, where students interrupt their yeshiva studies for service in the Israel Defense Forces. They believe that if a person ceases to learn Torah – even for a few months or years, and for a justified reason – he cannot become a *talmid chakham*, a Torah scholar. This ideology represents something of a diminished respect for Torah. The State of Israel prides itself on its scientists, doctors and intellectuals – the great majority of whom performed full military service. A great many of them even served as officers. They have attained impressive achievements in their respective fields, some even achieving international fame. I do not accept the argument that involvement in Torah is different, in this regard, from all other disciplines. Not all of the great Torah scholars of previous generations studied in *kollel*, and the occupation of Rabbi Yochanan the Shoemaker did not stand in the way of his greatness in Torah. I have had the privilege of serving as *Rosh Yeshiva* despite the fact that I "gave" the Nazis, may their memory be erased, more than half a year of my life. Afterwards, in a very different way, I performed my mandatory military service in the IDF for 16 months, aside from the months of reserve duty. Many of my contemporaries, rabbis who are greater than I, spent many long and difficult years in labor and concentration camps, yet today occupy an important place in the world of Torah. ["The Idea of the *Hesder* Yeshiva and Its Realization," *Alon Shevut Bogrim* 14 (5761), 35]

∽∘∾

There's a common phenomenon that characterizes a student's early days in the *beit midrash*. At first he is astounded at the scope and the great range of Torah, in all its levels: Halakha, Aggada, Tanakh. Sometimes he recoils in fear from this great fire. Like Ya'akov, he sees many stones before him, each calling to him, and it is as though they are arguing with each other and saying (*Chullin* 91b), "Let this *tzaddik* rest his head on me!" It takes some time until he finds the stone that suits his personality and abilities – whether in the sphere of in-depth study, or broad, "horizontal" coverage, or in the sphere of clarifying and organizing opinions. The same applies to the other areas of Torah, too – Tanakh or philosophy, as well as the ways of divine service in general: prayer, emphases in performing the commandments, the attitude towards communal affairs, ways of influencing and advancing the public.

["'On Aharon's Heart' – In Memory of Aharaleh Friedman, *z"l*," *Alon Shevut* 108 (5748), 3]

∽◦∾

People of my age – or close to my age – have a problem. For almost half a century we've been repeating the same things, performing them day in and day out, watching the same phenomena for years and getting used to it. Sometimes we think that things can't be changed, that that's how reality has to be. It's a fact: five, ten, twenty years ago things were the same. But when you come into contact with young, energetic people, there's nothing that is self-evident. They don't let us get used to a routine. They ask about every-thing – what's this, why is that, what is the justification for what we're doing? What psychological, experiential and intellectual basis is there for prayer and for the command-ments? These young people open a great gateway for their rabbis, and this only they are able to do, because for them nothing is self-evident. ["In Memory of David Cohen and Danny Moshytz, *Hy"d*," *Daf Kesher* 36 (5746)]

Sources and Resources

A World Built: Moshe Maya, *A World Built, Destroyed and Rebuilt: Rabbi Yehudah Amital's Confrontation with the Memory of the Holocaust*, transl. Kaeren Fish (Jersey City, 2004). Contains an appendix with three addresses by Rav Amital.

Jewish Values: R. Yehuda Amital, *Jewish Values in a Changing World*, ed. Amnon Bazak, transl. David Strauss (Jersey City, 2005).

Ha-Ma'alot mi-Ma'amakim: R. Yehuda Amital, *Ha-Ma'alot mi-Ma'amakim: Devarim be-Sugyot ha-Dor al ha-Teshuot ve-al ha-Milchamot* (Jerusalem, 1974).

All other sources are fully referenced inside.

Alon Shevut, *Alon Shevut Bogrim*, and *Daf Kesher* are Hebrew-language Torah periodicals of Yeshivat Har Etzion. *Alei Etzion* is the English-language Torah journal of Yeshivat Har Etzion.

Archives of *Daf Kesher* are available online: http://www.etzion.org.il/dk.
Archives of *Alei Etzion* are available online: http://www.haretzion.org/alei.htm.

Many other writings of Rav Amital are available online at Yeshivat Har Etzion's Israel Koschitzky Virtual Beit Midrash: http://www.vbm-torah.org/archive.htm.

For questions and comments about this book, please write to office@etzion.org.il.